Will You Still Need Me?

Will You Still Need Me?

Feeling Wanted, Loved, and Meaningful as We Age

Angela Browne-Miller

Foreword by Evacheska deAngelis

 PRAEGER

AN IMPRINT OF ABC-CLIO, LLC
Santa Barbara, California • Denver, Colorado • Oxford, England

Library of Congress Cataloging-in-Publication Data

Browne-Miller, Angela, 1952–
    Will you still need me? : feeling wanted, loved, and meaningful as we age / Angela Browne-Miller.
        p. cm.
    Includes bibliographical references and index.
    ISBN 978-0-313-35390-1 (alk. paper) — ISBN 978-0-313-35391-8 (ebook)
1. Aging—Psychological aspects 2. Older people—Psychology. I. Title.
    BF724.55.A35B76 2010
    155.6—dc22   2009051235

ISBN: 978-0-313-35390-1
EISBN: 978-0-313-35391-8

14 13 12 11 10   1 2 3 4 5

This book is also available on the World Wide Web as an eBook.
Visit www.abc-clio.com for details.

Praeger
An Imprint of ABC-CLIO, LLC

ABC-CLIO, LLC
130 Cremona Drive, P.O. Box 1911
Santa Barbara, California 93116-1911

This book is printed on acid-free paper ∞

Manufactured in the United States of America

To Lee and Louisa, and E. Lee

The Great Unfolding

By what truth
do we see truth.

By what eye
do we see
time passing.

By what thread
is woven
all we know
and
all we do not know
we know.

We are the
never ending stream
of all things
transforming through
life and time
to be in their own
life and time.

—Angela Browne-Miller

Contents

Foreword

This book opens a window into the hearts and minds of people of all ages—as we and they look at the aging process and at how individuals, families, and society treat aging. Offering a sensitive, up close, and personal bird's eye view into the firsthand experiences of persons interviewed for this book, aging unfolds into a deeply moving experience, one we all share. This is a particularly sensitive approach to the emotional and social aspects of doing the aging, watching the aging, and contemplating one's future as one ages.

This touching and incisive book is organized around Dr. Browne-Miller's years of research, and of working with clients of all ages, as well as interviews (of individuals of various ages) who have responded to interview questions regarding their feelings about aging in general and about: aging alone, living alone or with someone while aging or when older, being with someone not related to family versus being with family, having a significant other while aging—or not having one, self-perceptions as per aging, feelings about the future and about oneself as per the future, self-image as it relates to aging now and expected aging experiences, expectations of the aging experience, impressions of aging itself, and other emotional and social attitudes and perceptions as per the aging process.

The author of this book, Dr. Browne-Miller, weaves the findings of these interviews into a story-like, easy to follow, yet philosophical and research-based overview of, and dialog regarding, cross-generational concerns and feelings regarding aging. I do want to note that I have had the pleasure of assisting, along with others including the author herself, in the implementation of the final-round interview portion of this research. Simply having the opportunity to ask people of various ages and walks of life these questions, listed in Appendix A of this book, is an eye-opening experience. I come away more aware of what aging is about than I ever would have been without the opportunity to be involved in this work.

Through this sensitive, up-close-and-personal view of aging, something we all are doing every day of our lives, we see aging as a remarkable and quite touching experience—deeply disturbing for some, deeply rewarding for others, quite frequently both—an experience we all share.

Evacheska deAngelis

Preface

This book is a call for a new paradigm regarding: our aging processes, the meaning of aging itself, what being old in our society can be like, who the "old" are, who the "old" can be, how the "old" can see themselves and their journeys through their stages of life, and what new (or renewed) psychological and perhaps even spiritual (whether religious or nondenominational) perspectives can advance the experience of aging for all involved. It is my view that we can and must rethink aging, and completely revise our definitions of aging. We can envision and bring to fruition a whole new world for those in the last half, last third, or last quarter of their ever longer lives (as life spans are appearing to be increasing dramatically).

I am optimistic about the coming of new meaning to aging and to being old. Nevertheless, my touching pen to paper to write this book has been perhaps the most challenging for me so far, of all my book writings. It is not that words have failed me; I have not been at a loss for these words about aging. No, the words were and are still here, everywhere, ever present, flooding my mind. It is just that looking aging (as we define it today) in the eye can be rather difficult.

These words about growing older (and older) alone or lonely—or with company but perhaps still feeling more and more alone—lurk in many of our minds. Many of us ask ourselves the questions talked about in this book. And, many of us are in denial about the reality of aging itself, seeking to avoid the matter as it is truly playing out as long as we can. Looking aging in the face is not something at the top of our lists of longings, of desires, of wantings, and not central in our culture. It seems we close aging off from us as much as we can, locking the face of old age away as much as we can, living in a seemingly safe denial state, even as we age. This denial state is itself elusive, as even the denial of aging is denied. Even when we say we are recognizing aging in full, we may not be.

Still, aging is everywhere, happens to most everyone, is even part of most everyday lives. Not a day goes by when we are not growing at least a day older. Aging is a given. Few will debate this. Then why is saying what follows so challenging? Perhaps this is because this subject matter—even the question itself—*will you still need me?*—can be laden with so much latent emotion, so much buried stuff as yet unexpressed, silent, and lurking in the shadows. Aging is all around us and all within us, waiting in the wings, lurking in the shadows—or already taking place. Yet, all the while aging is so very in our faces, happening to us right before our very eyes, which we keep so very widely shut.

Aging is always clearly manifesting itself all around us, everywhere we look, and everywhere we cast our attention. Even when we choose to cast our attention away from aging, we have to see it. We have to feel the momentous progression of time through our lives—and of our lives through time.

Yet, it is not surprising that we shy away. After all, who will want to wonder: *will you, will anyone, still need me?* We do know what this wondering feels like. After all, who does not wonder exactly this at least once in her or his lifetime, if not regularly?

Angela Browne-Miller

Acknowledgments

I wish to acknowledge the hundreds of persons who participated in interviews for this book, *Will You Still Need Me?*, over a period of two years. It is from their hearts and minds that spring these themes of acceptance, anticipation, confusion, concern, and hope regarding aging, themes we all share. These are everyday people from all walks of life who took the time to step up and share their thoughts and feelings. (Interviewees, although not every one of you is quoted directly in this book, all of your comments are taken into account here. Thank you for your time, your honesty, your insights.)

I also want to thank my two research and interview assistants, Evacheska deAngelis and Cortney Johnson, who learned to conduct the final version of these interviews for this anecdotal study, and then did conduct many of these interviews themselves. Thank you, Evacheska and Cortney, for your dedication to this project and your great interviews.

So many colleagues and friends have stood and still stand by me through the chapters of life, and I thank every one of these persons. Here I want to specifically thank E. Lee Brazil for his undying loyalty and respect for the various projects I undertake. Lee, thank you for standing by me.

And I have to thank my parents, Lee and Louisa, both of whom passed on long before their time, and both of whom showed me how very precious every single moment of life, at any age, is. The value of one's life is indeed not to be measured in time or dollars, or in achievements, or in material goods acquired. The value is what we ourselves place as value on each of our own lives.

Note: The Stories Herein Are Our Stories

Hundreds of persons of all ages were interviewed for this book, over a two-year period. Quotes from many of these interviews are woven right into the text of this book. Additionally, 40 some specific interviews are captured here, in the form of numbered "stories" (e.g., Story 1, Story 2, and so on), with sets of these interviews found at the start of each of the six main parts of this book.

The profound commonality across these interviews is powerful, shouting even louder than words: We are all aging, we are all thinking (both consciously and subconsciously) about getting older, we are all watching others grow older. This reality is lost on no one, although there are those who would prefer to deny, ignore, or simply not see aging—yet.

These stories are our stories. These perspectives on and experiences of aging—or of looking ahead at aging—belong to all of us. You may see pieces of yourself or of someone you know here in one or more of these stories. You may find reading these stories, or at least some of these stories, to be an uplifting experience. You may find other stories rather sad, or even perhaps somewhat painful to read. Just consider yourself to be joining the dialog about growing older. You may indeed be sharing in the wondering: *will you still need me?*

Stories List

This chart lists the interviewee stories included in *Will You Still Need Me?*, in order of appearance in book. All names of interviewees have been changed. Most of these interviewee stories listed below have been merged with other of the interviewee stories collected for this book, and/or otherwise amended to further ensure the anonymity of the interviewees.

All narratives and quotes from interviewees have been thoroughly edited, adapted to fit this book, and even merged with comments by other interviewees whose stories are not formally included here to sharpen the points being made and also to further ensure confidentiality. Each of the resulting narratives (numbered stories listed here) are therefore built from many people's voices rather than one interviewee's voice. Also note that this is an exploratory, descriptive, and anecdotal form of research and no claim that this is a representative sample of any or all people of any or all age groups is made here.

Story Number	Name	Age	Gender
1	Dan W.	59	male
PART ONE			
2	Nona M.	27	female
3	Millicent D.	30	female
4	Andrea M.	34	female
5	Burton G.	29	male
6	Steven L.	32	male
7	Sharon J.	39	female
PART TWO			
8	Esmirelda Y.	38	female
9	Patricia V.	45	female
10	Devin P.	39	male
11	Greg T.	44	male
12	Barbara H.	38	female
13	Emily W.	47	female
14	Jeff B.	45	male
PART THREE			
15	Peter S.	49	male
16	Katy B.	45	female
17	George L.	51	male
18	Mark R.	56	male
19	Sally S.	52	female
20	Sandra M.	55	female
21	Geraldo H.	54	male
PART FOUR			
22	Marcia G.	64	female
23	Linda B.	62	female
24	Tom M.	56	male
25	Anton Y.	58	male
26	Ben D.	66	male
27	Jane Z.	60	female
28	Cristie S.	56	female
PART FIVE			
29	Arle H.	65	male
30	Arisha T.	65	female
31	Sten O.	68	male
32	Carla B.	67	female
33	Giselda A.	73	female
34	Rene M.	78	female
35	Walt M.	68	male
PART SIX			
36	Stanton Q.	89	male
37	Ida J.	84	female
38	Louis E.	87	male
39	Derrick G.	80	male
40	Lisa Lynn C.	77	female

Introduction

I have wanted to see life, death, and aging itself in a new way for much of my life. I have even longed for, felt my soul calling out for this new understanding of aging for much of my life. Having lost my parents long before their time, never really seeing them move into old age, I have felt that I understood death better than I understood aging, although most everyone I know has said that this is backward. What ever this drive, I do see that this interest I have in what it means to grow old in our world is a combination of personal and intellectual, social and psychological, and spiritual. The human spirit is confronted with a great question: Now that the human life span is growing far past older expectations, and now that the population of older persons is growing so dramatically—what do we do as we grow older—how do we make sense of the aging process—how do we make peace with aging, and even make aging the great adventure it can be?

Here, I have to recall an incident that relates to this matter of aging, and to the larger question of *will you still need me?*, for which this book is titled. One day many years ago, when I was a young adult, I had rented an old house in an old neighborhood with fellow college students. Our neighbors were a combination of students, professors, and then the older people who had lived in the neighborhood for decades. One of my neighbors was an elderly lady who lived alone. I sometimes visited her and took her cookies I had baked. One day, after I had been gone for several weeks, I visited this lady. She called "come in" from her living room. I walked in, said hello, and carried the dish of cookies I had brought her in to her kitchen.

This day, the kitchen was a bit messier than I remembered it. As I tried to put a few things away, I noticed that there were several dog food cans, some empty, some partially empty, on the counter. I was somewhat surprised that this lady would have suddenly gotten herself a dog, as she had said she did not like dogs on the several occasions I had mentioned the idea. So I called to the next room where she was sitting, "Where is your new dog?"

She replied, "What?"

"Your dog I said, your new dog."

"I don't have a dog," she answered.

"Well, then what is all this dog food doing in your kitchen?" I said. Silence.

I walked into the room where she was sitting and sat down in front of her. "OK, that's very funny. What do you mean? I mean, somebody's dog has been eating this dog food."

A few moments later, I was as sorry I could be that I had asked, and even sorrier about her response. She told me she had been eating that dog food because it had been a good buy and other canned food was getting too expensive.

An elderly woman, living alone in my neighborhood, being visited by no one but me so far as I could tell, was turning to dog food to eat. I was shocked. Although none of us had a great deal of money or good food to eat in those days, we had never had to turn to dog food the way this woman had. This began a long saga of my taking food over to her whenever I could, and of my seeking more information about her life, and especially about whatever family she might have somewhere. Eventually, her family appeared and moved her away, I assume into their home. However, they cut me off from all communication with this lady and I never knew what happened to her.

Whatever her story is, this is the story of so many of our elderly. And, this story, with all its questioning and unknowns, or something like it, could one day be the story for some of us. We do need a new way not only of seeing but also of responding to aging for ourselves—and for all those who have preceded us—and for all those who follow us into that phase of life.

Every one of us thinks about growing old. For some this is a far-off concept, while for others aging is occurring right now or in the not-so-distant future. Without a doubt, the average increase in life expectancies (and perhaps also in marriage breakups) will force many more individuals, families, friends (and employers and policy makers), to deal with the psychological (and economic and physical) factors of aging in general. With more people living longer, and with the population of older persons ever growing, we have to see aging whether we want to or not. Aging is signaling its reality everywhere around us (and within us). We have to look at aging in a new way. We need to find new understandings and definitions of aging, and new roles for our elders.

And right now, today, we have to see how many people are feeling less a part of the world over time, are feeling more and more alone, and or are anticipating being more and more alone. With so many actually being alone while aging and being alone when older, we have to see how many are looking at the possibility of spending, and or are already actually spending the last years of their lives alone. We cannot look away. We have to see this.

It is not that being alone is in itself a problem. Being alone is actually a state most preferred by some people; some actually do say they thrive on being alone. Yet what can (but does not always) accompany being alone in excess—troubling feelings such as isolation, loneliness, fear, agitation, confusion, disorientation, depression, despair—can pose serious problems. In these and related effects of some people being alone reside significant mental and physical health problems, plus threats to well-being and to a healthy longevity itself.

What signals might the mind send to the self when one is alone too much, especially as one ages? Could these signals even go so far as to tell the body that it is not necessary for it to function any longer—or at least to fully function any longer? Is there a message regarding perceived usefulness that is interpreted by one's biology? Is there a message regarding perceived usefulness that is interpreted by one's psychology?

Trying to touch this nerve, not to antagonize it, rather to know it and perhaps even sooth it, I have written *Will You Still Need Me: Feeling Wanted, Loved, and Meaningful as We Age*. This book is built upon hundreds of interviews (conducted in three rounds) with individuals of various ages who have responded to questions regarding their views on aging. (See Appendix A for the final interview questionnaire—the list of questions used in the last round of interviews conducted for this anecdotal study.) From these interviews, these people's stories, I have selected 40 to report herein, labeling these Story #1, Story #2, and so on. Where I refer to these interviews, or cases, the names have been changed. Most geographic and other identifying factors are left out so that primarily the age and gender of the person or persons referred to in these stories are identified. In some cases, several of these interviews are combined in the interest of further anonymity. Although not all interviewees requested anonymity, all have been provided it herein.

The interviewees have offered their unguarded thoughts regarding their own and others' aging processes. The stories these interviewees point to and frequently elaborately discuss, address the social and emotional aspects of, and attitudes toward, aging including: watching aging; contemplating one's own aging; aging with a significant other—or alone; and what it might be like to have no one, no companion, family, or friend left to share life with. (In fact, talk about losing friends as one ages is common among the older interviewees.)

Other aspects of aging and of being alone are also talked about by these interviewees as they tell their stories. Among these aspects of aging and perceptions of aging are: growing physical pain and even disability, and related concerns about being alone and or not needed; job loss or other employability issues and what this might mean about being needed, wanted, or cared about; other economic crises and how these might impact aging and companionship while aging; and divorce in midlife or in later life and how this might affect the aging experience. Numerous other issues were raised during these interviews, including but not limited to: What might happen if one has left behind earlier in life one's primary religion and or philosophy, and then finds that not having this to turn to in later life can be problematic (which it apparently is for some but not all people).

These *Will You Still Need Me?* interviewees reveal their self-perceptions, their feelings about the future, their self-images as these relate to aging, and their expectations and impressions of aging itself. Many interviewees also share their concerns that with aging comes not only possible loneliness, but also possible meaninglessness and even uselessness. On the other hand, some of the older interviewees talk about how they more than ever value their lives, every moment of their lives, and even find spiritual growth in aging.

Do not be surprised if you feel you know one or more of these interviewees. Their stories are our stories, or our parents' stories, or the stories of family members, friends, colleagues, neighbors, people next to us on the bus, people in the streets. There is an undeniably universal nature to the aging experience, and to the experience of looking ahead at one's own aging, and around oneself at the aging of others. We all hear ourselves and others ask the perennially asked and almost entirely unspoken question: *will you still need me?* After all, few want to reveal to others, let alone to themselves that, somewhere deep, deep down inside, they wonder, they have to wonder: Will anyone still need me when I am old? Will the world still need me when I am old?

This book brings together the findings of these interviews with contemporary research regarding the aging process. *Will You Still Need Me?* is not a review of current research. Rather this book invites the reader (in fact it invites readers of all ages) into a dialog regarding aging and how it looks, how it feels, what it means to those watching and to those experiencing it.

This book is not to add to the pain already so present in this world, nor to paint a bleak and one-sided picture of aging. Instead, the goal here is to unmask the ever looming ghost, to paint in daylight color the less than visible, to point to the huge yet little acknowledged elephant in the room: The enormity of the importance of being needed, needed by someone—by society, or by a community, or by a coworker, or by a mate, or by a friend, or by a neighbor, or by a pet, or even by a plant, or even perhaps—an idea we return to at the close of this book—*by oneself*. For whether I will still need me, *whether you will still need you,* is perhaps the greatest question of them all.

Story #1

Dan W., Age 59

Dan W., age 59, lives part time on the Native American reservation where he grew up, and works in a city 100 miles away a few days a week. He lives on the "rez" as he calls it with his family. He says he is very close to the people of his community. "We are really all family here," he says.

When asked what he thinks about growing old, and whether he thinks he will feel needed by his family and community when he is old, Dan W. answers a definite yes: "Yes. We don't worry about whether we will be needed when we are older people. My people are not like the people out there who do not have respect for their elders. My people, well we know we will be needed. We get more and more important as we age. We know more. Our elders are the carriers of our wisdom." Dan W. speaks of his elders with great reverence and immediately wants to make clear that the elders are "the ones who are wise, their wisdom guides everyone else. They know what the young do not yet know. . . . But this does not say that we do not need the young people too, we need the young very much."

At this point in the interview, Dan W. waves his arm toward the cemetery that is built right there, near the center of his community. "Look here. See these graves. Most of these are for little children. We have lost so many of them before they grow up, even before they make it through childhood. Children are special because they become older people, and in time, they become our elders. We still need them. We need our children and we need our elders. Our children are our future, and our future elders. So when we cherish the young people, we cherish the old people. They are the future. And the people who cherish the young people most are our elders, because they know this best."

I

~∞~

TOUCHING THE
TENDER ISSUE
OF AGING

Why is it that the Lion's strength weakens to nothing?
—Jalāl ad-Dīn Muḥammad Rūmī

Seeing Ourselves Growing Older. Photo courtesy of U.S. Administration on Aging, via PINGNEWS.

Story #2

Nona M., Age 27

Nona M. is a 27-year-old, single woman. Nona M. has never been married and has no children. She lives in a big city with two female roommates. Nona M. says that whenever she thinks about getting older, she thinks about marriage. She adds, "Marriage is very important to me. I want to find the person I know I will be able to spend my time with when I get old."

Nona M. works for a corporation "doing digital art," and although she is "only in my late 20s," she says that already the wrist pain and carpal tunnel syndrome she has developed while on this job concerns her, and causes her to wonder "what aging holds in store" for her. She worries that "it will get worse as I get older, and lead to more serious problems." But simultaneously, "this is all I know how to do." Nona M. says she doesn't know if or how she could ever be able to find another career path. She is concerned that she will not have enough money when she is "old" if she cannot save enough money for her old age, "starting right now." And, she feels that her career path is "the only way I will be able to make money and save it."

Nona M. emphasizes again and again that when she thinks about getting older, she also always thinks "family and children." She says she also thinks about her career and its direction. She says that she used to think 40 was old, but the closer she gets to 30, the more 40 seems "not so old. I don't know at what age I'll consider myself old. Maybe 50 or maybe 70. Hopefully I won't be old 'til I'm in my 80s."

Nona M.'s greatest concerns about getting older are also what she views as the positive aspects of aging. She wants to make sure to "settle down and have a family, because I think that is also the best part about getting older, being able to have those things." She says she has never been divorced, and that her more serious relationships have lasted only a couple of years each, at most—"and then there is always the breakup. It's like we put all this time into building a relationship to get us through the rest of our lives, and then there it goes. Sadly, building something that will last into old age sounds almost impossible to me."

Nona M. says that the relationship breakups she has experienced were actually fueled by her thoughts about growing older, and that she actually ended the relationships because she "knew they weren't the person I'd want to see every day in my 80s." Nona M. has no children. "I hope that one day, my children will be able to take care of me and my future husband by living close to us and seeing us often." Nona M. has no grandparents and her parents have not required her care, but she says "if they needed me, I'd always take care of them."

Finding herself "all alone" as she gets older is indeed a strong concern for Nona M. However, at the same time, she says she does "not presently give a lot of thought to the subject of aging itself." Nona M. explains that she doesn't give much thought to her friends' aging either, "or to any other people's aging in general. . . . It's not that I don't care, it's just that I never really think about it. I just don't want to think about it. It's not a happy thought. . . . But I must be thinking about aging at least a bit because I already know who the Godparents of my future children will be. That's thinking about being a bit older, isn't it?"

Nona M., at age 27, appears to be quite focused on setting a strong foundation for her life by "finding a man and starting a family with him. This way, I'll always have company and people to need me." Nona M. concludes her interview by reemphasizing that her largest concerns about aging are wondering whether she will "ever manage to find a life partner, someone to go through the years with, or whether I will have to do this getting old thing all alone," and how her career will affect her health as time goes by as "if I can't work, if I can't take care of myself—then no one will want me, ever."

Story #3

Millicent D., Age 30

Millicent D. is a 30-year-old single female who works in retail management. She is the mother of two. While she has never been married, in the
past year she "split with the father" of her youngest child, with whom she
was "with for over eight years, eight years too long I think, as it used up
time I needed to find someone else, I guess." Millicent D. took her two
children and moved in with her parents after her "tumultuous" breakup.

Millicent D. only recently turned 30. She laments "not being in my 20s
anymore. My 20s were the time for finding out what I wanted and who I
wanted in life. But I sort of missed that boat, or picked wrong. But I know
there still is time. I mean I'm not old yet." Millicent D. says she does "not
really think about aging very often.... The different age groups and the
signs of aging don't mean very much to me right now, not yet I guess."
However, she does "think about something related to aging, because I
know that I want to find a man who will fit in with my lifestyle and be
happy with my two children from my previous relationships sometime
soon. Definitely before I'm 40. Now that is old, 40. Yes, 40! Yikes." Another aging related matter (as Millicent D. sees it, aging related that is)
that is very important to Millicent D. is buying a home "before I'm 40."
40 is the age that Millicent D. thinks of as "finally grown up, settled, and
responsible. Or else. You see, if you don't have things figured out by then,
well then, you are getting too old to start."

Upon further reflection, sometime into this interview, Millicent D. decides she is indeed concerned about aging even now, at her age of 30. After the recent break up of her "eight plus year relationship," she is left with "concerns about growing older," because she does want "someone to share my life with as I get older. I don't want to be alone. I really don't. And I could end up alone later on. But right now, I don't feel alone with my kids around. They keep me busy, for sure. In fact, I'm never alone."

Millicent D. says she hasn't given any thought to whether her children will take care of her when she gets older, if need be. She has never had to care for a parent or grandparent, and does not have "a model for this." Millicent D.'s parents "still work and will for several decades I think. It is good they are out there as a backup for me in my weird life. I don't want them getting real real old yet, I like them the way they are right now. And, I admit, I still need them to help me. I really need them to take care of me, not the opposite, not yet. Not for a long time. I hope that doesn't sound selfish."

Economic stresses play a large part in Millicent D.'s thoughts about getting older because she wants to be a "financially stable adult. I thought I would be one by now.... I also worry about Social Security and Medicare, because I think these things will not exist by the time I am eligible for them. That's why I need financial stability soon, so I can be ok when I get old...I really look forward to retirement. If only I could do it now! But young people probably get bored if they don't work, and I like my job." Millicent D. sees her life as something still in formation, with enough time to resolve the emerging emotional and social and financial questions she is finding she has about aging.

Millicent D. feels she is typical of her peers in that "none of us think about getting real old, like 80 or 90, very much right now. In fact, we don't even think about being 40 or 50 or 60. If it weren't for a few of our relationships and marriages breaking up, and some of us now being single mothers, we probably wouldn't think about aging at all right now. I think marriage and relationship break ups make young people think about aging more."

Story #4

Andrea M., Age 34

Andrea M. is a 34-year-old female in a long-term relationship with the man she "lives with." They have been together for 10 years. She is currently employed in "IT" (intelligence technology she explains) for a corporation. When Andrea M. thinks about getting older, she really wants to own a house. She says that "this whole thing about aging makes me want to know, to be sure that I will have some place that's my own to live in when I get old. I want that place now. I want that certainty now, so I won't have to worry about it when I get older." To Andrea, "anything over 75 qualifies as old."

Andrea M. has never been divorced or experienced a major relationship breakup. She has no children and she doesn't want any in the future. Therefore, concerns about her children taking care of her in the future "don't apply to me. I guess I'm on my own!...How does this feel to me? Well, right now, it doesn't seem like a big deal. It is what is, that's all." Andrea M. helps to take care of her mother, who is in her late 50s, by sending her money every month. She is the first person in her family to have graduated from college and have a strong income, so she feels "like it's my duty to help out my mom. It's because I can." But she doesn't see this as getting older or more mature, it's just her duty and her "ability" as she calls it.

While Andrea M. doesn't appear very excited about the relationship she's been in for the past 10 years, she doesn't want to end it because, "I don't want to be alone when I get old. I don't even want to be alone now. Alone is such an ugly word to me. Anything but alone." Andrea M. says that being alone "has an icky, depressing feeling to it."

Being alone is clearly a concern for Andrea M. She is also concerned about several health conditions as she gets older. Heart disease and other conditions do run in her family. She makes sure to get regular health checks often to watch for these problems. Andrea M. voices a concern that "the family is quite tired after all the many family illnesses. No one can handle it if anyone else gets sick now. Guess I will stay well. I have to. No one needs another one of us needing help and attention."

Economic issues don't seem to be a concern for Andrea M. as she is happy with her current income and the pay structure at her company. She likes her benefits and feels that her income is securing her for the future. Andrea M. says that she has "never before this interview wondered whether my present financial situation and income, and my financial independence, will last forever or not. This is a disturbing thing to think about. I'm not sure anyone can help me out if I need help, not now and certainly not when I am old. This is scary, real scary. It's really too much for me to think about clearly, I can't think about this, not right now."

Andrea M. draws upon the experiences of her peers. "We are all wondering about our futures, this is for sure. We just don't talk about it much, and we try to push the thoughts back. Why have the thoughts and problems of being old when young, it just makes being old come sooner. Being old does not look so good, so who wants it early?"

Burton G., Age 29

Burton G. is a 29-year-old single male. Burton G. currently lives with his mother and father as he recently moved home to help his mother in her recovery from cancer. Burton G. currently works in the photography department of a large corporation. Burton G. recently turned 29. He didn't give aging much thought until he realized, "Man, I only have one more year left in my 20s." He can't explain what seems different to him between one's 20s and one's 30s, but "it does concern me. I don't really want to be old. Old sounds pretty awful." To Burton G., old means "OLD. Like, 90s is OLD. But the 30s is old enough, gee."

Burton G. does say that there are "some positive aspects of growing older. People my age think getting older is a good thing. Well maybe not real, real old, like 90, but 35 and 45 are good. I mean that an older person, well maybe not real old, but older than I am now, can get more respect from people. And getting older can mean developing more in my career, which is in a competitive industry. More time under my belt doing what I do, and the older I am, the better I will be seen by the people I work with. I don't like being the youngest one at work. . . . It makes me feel like I am at the bottom of the list, which I am."

Burton G.'s greatest concerns about getting older are health concerns. Several different types of cancer run in both sides of his family. Burton G. himself has already dealt with a bout of skin cancer. Due to his family history, Burton G. gets screened for different types of cancer twice a year.

He worries that "the older I get, the more afraid I am of getting cancer. So many people in my family have had it more than once, or had more than one kind of it. It usually hit them in their 40s and so being in my 40s scares me. It seems like being in the 40s is both good and scary."

Burton G. has "never been divorced or even in a long-term relationship." He wants a family one day, but feels that he is "too young, at least emotionally, to even *think* about kids right now. Being young like me means I can be selfish, not think too much about anyone but myself, and kids would end that for me. I'll have kids when I'm older." Burton G. believes his future children "will one day take care of me, for sure, because I've set the stage by taking care of my parents when they need me." Burton G. hasn't really thought much about being alone when he gets older. He says he is presently "more concerned about having kids some day than about having a life partner in my 80s. That is a bit far away for me to get yet."

The economy "worries me, because it could be eating all chances of Social Security and Medicare for my generation. Not really sure what's going to happen with that. I just hope my generation can survive when we get old. We don't really have a contingency plan. We're going to really have to depend on each other as we get older, because there won't be much else for us to count on. The government sure won't be taking care of us, because it will be broke. I guess we'll need each other a whole lot then."

Burton G. explains, "Most people my age, at least my friends, think that when we get old we will have to take care of ourselves because society will cop out on us. They won't have jobs for us, and they won't have Social Security for us. Then what? Welfare? We just aren't sure what the long range future looks like. This makes us act a bit crazy, like there is no tomorrow."

Story #6

Steven L., Age 32

Steven L. is a 32-year-old male, who has been in a "committed relation-ship," as he describes it, for nine years. He lives with his "best girlfriend ever" as he calls her. Steven L. works in sales for a small hi-tech company. He says he does "not want to get older. Turning 30 was awful for me. I don't even like celebrating birthdays. I don't feel old, because I don't feel the number that goes with my age. Sometimes I feel like I'm still a teenager." When asked what years "old" is to him, Steven L. says "each decade seems old. 30s seemed old. In fact, they still do. 40s is ancient, and anything above that just seems super old." Steven L. says his biggest concerns about getting older are "being OLD. But also being financially stable. That's really important to me." When asked what the positive as-pects of getting older might be, he says "marrying my girlfriend and start-ing a family. We really want kids."

Steven L. has never been divorced, or left a long-term relationship. He does not know what a "serious breakup of a relationship that leaves me all alone would feel like. Doesn't sound good. I think that loneliness hurts and I wouldn't like it. I wouldn't live through it." Steven L. adds that he hopes to have children and that his children will be successful, and will-ing to take care of him when he gets older, even though he has never had the responsibility of helping a parent or grandparent himself. Steven L. emphasizes that one thing he does not want is "to be alone when I get old.

I definitely don't want to be alone *and* be old. That combination would be pretty bad I think."

Steven L. wishes that someone had helped him "with my finances more when I was in my 20s. Having a financial foundation as you get old is so important, I wish I'd been able to start saving for the future earlier. I wonder if I will have the benefit of Social Security because our economy is so messed up. It's like we're all getting older and older *and older* and there is nothing solid to take care of us out there at the end, not even ourselves." Steven L. also says he hopes to be able to retire at an age that he is still able to travel the world and "see lots of great things. I hope I won't be too old when I finally can."

"I think most of my friends are worried that when it is finally time for us to have a lot of fun and freedom, we won't be able to. So we believe we should get at least some fun in the now, along the way to old age. But I do think that there are things to look forward to, good things about getting older. I think it is a good idea to try to look forward to things, so we can feel good about getting older. Thinking there is something great waiting for us is reassuring."

However, Steven L. adds that he and his friends are increasingly "scared about the future, what with global warming and nuclear weapons and terrorism.... I think I'm trying to say that we wonder if we will be able to get old, if there will be a world for us to get old in."

Story #7

Sharon J., Age 39

Sharon J. is a single 39-year-old female. She is the mother of two and is divorced. She currently lives with her boyfriend of three years. Sharon J. is an attorney. She seems to have dedicated a lot of her spare time to not getting older. "I stay really active, and I like to go dancing. I don't feel old, so I'm not old. Even though I'll be 40 next year. If you don't feel old then you are not old because old is just a state of mind." When asked what age or ages represent getting older, Sharon J. says, "I think age is relative. I hope I'll never be old. Anyway, I am not going to say I am old someday, I just won't."

Sharon J. has been divorced but says, "I'm happy I did it when I did. I wouldn't want to keep getting older and be with someone I didn't want to be with. Also I think breaking up a relationship gets harder as you get older." She says she hasn't "given much thought" to her children taking care of her when she is a lot older. She has never had to take care of a parent or grandparent. She says "being alone isn't really an issue for me. I like to have my boyfriend around, but I like my alone time too. I don't know if that will change as I age. I think I will always like my alone time, at least I hope so."

Sharon J. has "already beaten breast cancer twice," so while diseases concern her, she says "this issue has nothing to do with aging." Her first bout of breast cancer came "in my 20s. Obviously it had nothing to do with age."

Sharon J. hopes to retire "when I'm in my late 50s, because I want to have fun. My kids will be adults then and I'll be able to do what I want to do. It seems I get the best of it all, as I get to have the kids and raise them, and then still be young enough to play after that. I like play. I think life needs play. More time to play is the part of getting older that I like."

Commentary

The stories of the people interviewed for this book represent a dialog among ourselves regarding aging. These stories also represent our dialog with aging itself. We talk to aging, we ask aging what it has in store for us, we want to know what part of the aging process we can have a say in. How much of what is happening to us, and how much of what will happen to us is out of our control?

Here, in the first part of this book, we have considered the stories of several people who have distinct views regarding aging. For example, in Story 1, Dan W., age 59, shares his community's special understanding of the value of elders and their wisdom. For Dan W., everything to respect and protect the elders is essential. And, protecting the children so that they one day become the elders of the community is also essential. This reverence for the elders is so powerful that Dan W. does not fear aging, and rather looks forward to the opportunity, respect, status, and great meaning he feels aging offers.

Following Story 1, we hear from five interviewees whose ages range from 27 to 34, and then in Story 7, hear from a 39-year-old. (Story 7 of 39-year-old Sharon J. is included with this set of stories to provide a contrast to the other stories in this first set, and also to show a distinct continuity from story to story and age range to age range.) These interviewees speak of the general importance of marriage in the now, as having company and the presumed social status of marriage is desired. However, marriage is also desired from the standpoint of looking ahead at aging, planning ahead (or attempting to plan ahead) for aging. Several of these interviewees express concerns regarding whether they will have someone to grow older and then old with. So important is having a relationship with someone they can spend the rest of their lives with, that one of these persons, Nona M. in Story 2, has left several relationships she knew she did not want to have be with her on a long-term basis, people she did not want to grow older with. We could say she chose to be alone in the now, if she had to be, in favor of, in search of, a mate she could share time with in the future. In this sense, her priorities are being acted on.

Several of these interviewees specify that they do want children, as this is part of the family they want to have when they get older. They expect that these children will be around to provide company and to care for them as they age, if need be. Again, the desire to have children in the now may be important, however what is being expressed by several of these interviewees is that children will be important parts of their lives as they grow older.

Concerns about finding a mate, about earning a living, about having enough money to be comfortable at this stage of life as well as in older age are voiced by these interviewees. However, thinking about aging itself is for several of these people not a high priority, and or something they are not comfortable thinking about. For most of these interviewees, the ages 80 and 90 are very old. However, anything over 40, 50, or 60 is also at least somewhat old. "Old" itself is still a far away factor, and present time issues are more front and center stage, perhaps as they should be. Overall, among this group, there is a vague denial of the reality of aging, and certainly a need for greater understanding of what aging is.

Also of note is the comment made my Steven L. in Story 6 that concerns about the future—and about whether there will even be a future—mount as ecological and geopolitical pressures appear to mount. How does this looming concern—*will there even be a future to grow old in*—affect young adult's views of aging, and even of their present time lives?

1

⊙⊗⊙

Growing Up and Up and Up

Let's go back to childhood for a moment. Children have about as many views of aging as do people of all other ages. They see all around them that things, living things, as well as inanimate objects, such as toys, equipment, and books get old. Computers, papers, crayons wear down and get old. And people: people do get old! This is so obvious to the young that in fact they look at anything over the teenage years as old and anything over 30 or 40 as quite old.

Young people do see living things get old, pets get old, people get old. In fact, many young people consider just about everything that is not within 10 or 15 years of their own ages as already old or in the process of getting old. At very young ages, children can even think age seven is old, or even age five—kindergarten age, or even any age a little older than a child's own age.

The concept that "death follows old age" is quite a profound concept for anyone let alone a very young person to assimilate on her or his own, deep within her or himself. Yet even death is everywhere, and young people do see that pets, insects, even people, do die. Death is always there, always out there. Yet, for many young people, this will not be an entirely conceivable reality until many decades later. When is it that we are finally able to understand death? Perhaps never. Still, it looms out there, beyond aging. The sequence—grow up, grow on, grow on and on, grow older, grow old, grow quite old, then just disappear or die—comes into focus as children grow. Slowly, the notion that there is a life span—and that this life span has a beginning, a middle, a later phase, and an end—surfaces. Until then, children tend to think of those children who are growing up (and up) as separate from adults who appear to be doing something else.

Somehow, in the young mind, death can become a reality before aging itself becomes a reality. Still, as we grow, death remains vague, a great unknown. Aging becomes increasingly clear to us. Death does not. We can see what happens during the aging process, and we cannot see what happens after death. For all the unknowns or uncertainties past the point of actual physical death, the realities of aging are all too fathomable—especially once we realize that we are always aging.

After growing up, and gaining an initial foothold on adulthood, aging may tend to emerge in our minds as something less than wonderful, perhaps even not entirely desirable. Aging eventually leads to growing older, old, and then very old. As children, what we see of old age is something we may accept in other people but do not want for ourselves. We do not even fathom ourselves as ever being very old. When we are very young, old age is something happening to other people; we rarely if ever actually think about ourselves as ever being old, very old. We see old age as belonging to old people—at most, a vague and distant reality for ourselves.

Yet old age itself is changing right before our eyes. Old definitions of "old" are shifting in our times. Even middle age years are changing. Middle age years are extending later and later; and then old age begins later and later. It is only a matter of years now before people over 65 are a larger population than people 5 and under. This is the first time in the history of the human species that this is taking place. Old age will take on not only new meaning but new proportions.

Yes, old age looks different these days—and lasts longer and longer. And this does not have to be a bad thing. The possibilities that the even longer periods of time we will be alive and will be enjoying life are growing. Aging is slowly taking on a new face. So while we do grow up and then up and up, we now will be finding ourselves growing up and up and up on and on and on ...

2

When Is Getting Older Aging?

When do young people realize that they are indeed always aging? Perhaps not during youth when aging is simply called "growing up." It will be many, many years later when the generation now growing up realizes that it has begun to grow "down" or at least to grow older, or old.

Even the phase I describe so lightly here, growing down—or growing on and then down—or whatever we want to call the process of not growing as quickly or perhaps not growing at all—does not explain aging. Even seeing others get older does not explain aging. Even aging itself does not explain aging. Maybe nothing explains aging so well as actually living the process, as actually finding—or expecting to someday find—oneself "getting older," or perhaps better stated, "growing older."

Growing older itself might appear to be a huge, massive, even arduous undertaking from the young end of the lifetime spectrum all the way to the other far off end of the lifetime spectrum—were it to be seen step by step all the way through. Again, one might say: what hard work just getting from the age of 1 to the age of 100! However, few at the young end of the lifetime spectrum are actually looking ahead carefully. It might be decades upon decades upon decades before they experience advancing age let alone advancing old age. It might be old age before they recognize the increments of aging that they are indeed experiencing, living though. Or it might be never. As we see from what many of our older interviewees (many of whose interviews have been summarized in later chapters of this book) have told us, old age "just sort of sneaks up on you," and "it doesn't say, 'hello here I am getting you older...'"

While they may long for the privileges that the "big kids" get and that the grownups seem to own, very young people do not crave the experience of aging itself. Nor do many of them imagine what this experience might actually feel like. Instead, *growing up to growing older to being old* is something others—people out there in the world—or even others near them—are having happen to them. However, what it actually feels like to grow old it is not truly imagined for what it will truly be like when it truly takes place. Everything outside of being old is outside of being old. That is, until you are on the inside looking out, on the inside of being old looking out at the world in which you are old.

Moving from childhood into adulthood, we see how young adults in their 20s and those in their 30s (as in Stories 2 through 6 at the start of part one of this book—and also in Story 7, the perspective of a 39-year-old) have quite practical attitudes regarding aging, are even sensitive to aging issues, yet are quite distant from the reality of the process of aging. For the most part, adults in their 20s and 30s think about aging from a distance and only occasionally. At this stage of life, aging is not here until aging comes: it's out there, somewhere, but not right now—and this is fine.

3

⊸⊶⊷⊸

The Desire Not to See Aging

"Yikes," some of the younger adults say when asked about aging. Many of the young adults (in their 20s and early 30s) participating in this study actually change their minds about being interviewed for *Will You Still Need Me?* when finally actually being asked about aging itself. "Oh wait, right now? We are talking about this right now? Ummm....I really don't want to think about getting old. Not today. I'm sorry, I know I said I would talk to you about all this, but I just realized that I don't really want to do this interview." Several of them added comments such as "it's just too painful" and "it's all so heavy, why think about this right now" and "I care about old people, like my grandparents for example, or my parents too, I guess I really do care, but I just can't talk about getting old that much. I hope you don't mind."

Of course, when confronted with this response, I just smile and say, "Sure, I understand, its OK. And thank you anyway." Yet, I am receiving valuable information in even these responses (or nonresponses) to my questions about perceptions of aging. In a nutshell, these young adults are revealing to us the elephant in the room, the large animal we all on some level deny the existence of—the sometimes seeming beast we call aging. After all, whether we can face aging head on, or whether we would rather simply deny it—especially our own aging—speaks directly to the question of *will you still need me?* The truth is, we don't want to wonder too much whether we will still be needed or wanted in old age. We don't even know or want to know whether we will still need ourselves.

What is it about the face of aging we can have such a hard time looking into? It is the mirroring of ourselves now or later that we see there? Is it the reminder that none of us who live out the average life span of our times will escape getting older? Is it that we secretly harbor the wish that getting older will not lead to aging, or to any of the challenges so commonly associated with aging?

Is it that no matter what is done to stop the clock, time continues on?

Time. Time and denial. These phenomena go together. In that aging is both a physical process and a psychospiritual process, denial is a powerful component of the process. Denial is a not seeing of aging. Denial is a denying that aging takes place, and that it can happen to us.

This denial is so very powerful that it can blind us to what is right before our eyes: the population over 65 is growing rapidly at the same time the average life span is extending. However many older persons we do see around us today, this subset is expanding virtually exponentially. Still, the desire not to see aging runs even deeper than the obvious not seeing of aging so natural at younger ages. There is an active denial mechanism at work here, actively protecting the self from seeing what may be future loneliness, and perhaps future pain and suffering, or at least old age, which is different from young age.

Leading a life aimed at surviving in the now can involve not allowing oneself to see that there may be something less than entirely desirable out there in the future. Think of a road, a road you have to choose to drive down. If you think that the trip may not be desirable, or at least not as desirable as the present, will you take that road? Maybe, however, the choice to move forward involves having some hope that forward is alright, not bad, maybe even good. Now, where the road is growing older, the road is inevitable. So instead of not choosing the road, there is a denial regarding what may be ahead on that road.

4

⸺◦∞◦⸺

What Aging Is (Or Is It?)

If we wanted to, we could simply describe aging as the aging of the body. After all, there is a distinctly physical component to aging. There is the natural aging of many physical functions: the declines in the efficiency of the heart muscle that then pumps blood less efficiently; the fatty deposits that may collect in the arteries that can then harden the arteries; the natural loss of elasticity of the arteries that, along with the decreased power of the heart as a pump, can lead to high blood pressure. Other changes that can come with age include changes in the digestive system, the sensory system (ears, eyes, nose, tongue), and changes in the skin. Then there are the weakening of the bones, and the stiffening of the ligaments. Muscles can lose strength and flexibility with age. Reflexes can grow slower and reaction time can decrease.

And then there is the brain. The brain does lose neurons, and this in itself represents some degree of brain loss. The neurons themselves can also decrease in efficiency. The aging brain is an aging brain, and must be regarded as such. However, the brain does compensate for the loss of neurons and any decreased efficiency of neurons, at least to some extent, by forming new connections. And here is the power of the brain to affect the aging curve, to make a difference in the aging experience. (We return to this notion in later chapters.)

Aging is a tricky thing. On the one hand aging is right there, in our faces, and on the other hand, aging—what it is, what it really is—is about as elusive as anything can be. We cannot touch aging, we cannot bottle it, nor can science (thus far) give us a shot to truly prevent it. Our cells carry within them coding to die, and these cells obey this coding. Aging is simply part of the program. Perhaps, were we to know the designer of our programming better, we would comment to that designer that aging is a bizarre and even cruel form of planned obsolescence. Why do this to us? Similar to new makes and models of automobiles, planned obsolescence builds in an aging process, a guaranteed wear-down effect. And, where this effect is not working very well, not wearing models down rapidly enough, planned obsolescence offers a means of forcing the old make and model into a perceived state of being suddenly or eventually old-fashioned.

There is a quixotic and dual nature, a sort of relentlessly tricky two-faced aspect, to aging. On the one hand, there is the universal experience of aging shared by all living things, by all of us. Aging is something that is not only natural but also a given, a movement through time. And, with the gift of time, with the time of one's life we know is promised to all those who live out the length of the life span typical of their times—their comes aging. That is that. All roads lead to the same place. No way out. (Not yet, science may tell us. Someday but not yet.)

Yet aging, as it moves belligerently through time, has also a stationary nature, a quality of motionlessness, even a timelessness. Life may speed by more and more rapidly, with every day another piece of life already lived never to be lived again. However, concurrently, there is also a sense of suspended timelessness, a sense of floating in a vague limbo—or at least the feeling of lost or maybe motionless time. Where did that moment go? How did this day go by? What happened today? Anything? In the moments and seconds and minutes and hours and days and weeks and months and years and decades of growing older, as age increases time as it is perceived both slows and races by.

Where the commonalities of aging—the things about aging we all face or may face—are virtually inescapable, on certain levels the individual experiences aging *alone* regardless of how many people she or he is surrounded by or in contact with. No one can live in any one particular aging body along with anyone else. In this sense, aging is a solo journey. Certainly most people will experience some similar highs and lows or parallel joys, pleasures, rewards, loves, and losses, fragilities, imbalances, tirednesses, sleeplessnesses, losses of focus, creaks or aches, and so on. However, no single experience of aging is replicated exactly in another being. Each of us follows our own path of aging.

Knowing, really knowing, what is taking place in the mind and heart and body of the aging spouse, lover, partner, friend, family member—parent, grandparent, or child—is never entirely possible. We are always outside the whole and the full detail of someone else's aging experience. We can only think we know the physical, mental, emotional, and spiritual processes someone else is undergoing.

For this reason, while there is the overwhelming yet somewhat denied universality in all aging, there is also perhaps equally overwhelming yet denied solitariness in aging. In some sense, we must acknowledge that in many ways, each of us comes in alone and goes out alone.

5

⸎

Companionship and the Prospect of Aging

The majority of persons interviewed for *Will You Still Need Me?* emphasize that having companionship in older age is (or will be) quite important to them. Clearly, the human being is a social animal who generally leads, where it can, a social life. Given that living in families, communities, and societies are social activities and even social processes, the majority of, if not all, human beings do have a social component to their lives. Add in common activities such as work, entertainment, politics, sports, and perhaps even shopping and other more mundane aspects of life, and virtually everywhere we turn we find some degree of social engagement taking place. We might also say that most people's lives take place *immersed* in social settings, and that the social environment in all its forms is a sort of medium or atmosphere in which we swim just to live—it is our habitat. (See chapters 11 and 12 for more on this.)

Companionship is generally important at all ages. Most people seek companions, and are sad when they do not have them or lose them. This is because this thing we call companionship provides something we may need for survival—a fundamental form of social engagement. From a survival standpoint, companionship has its virtues. Having someone to talk to is not only nice sometimes, it is actually a means of keeping the mind engaged in life, interacting with the world. We have all heard the "use it or lose it" saying, however we may not see how this applies to social interacting—human relations and relating. We may not realize that social interaction—with one or more persons—is a form of exercise—and that close companionship offers a profound form of exercise. Certainly, this interacting is a form of psychological or mental exercise rather than of physical exercise; however, the line between these domains blurs. After all, most social interaction has a physical component, and even can have physical health effects.

Where does companionship actually come in here? We do not need companionship to be afforded opportunities to interact with people. It is relatively easy to dose oneself with at least one interaction with another person per day—even if just by going to the food store and paying for one's food, or asking a stranger on the street a question, or perhaps being stopped for a traffic law violation and conversing with the officer ticketing you. However, there is a qualitative difference between interacting with a stranger, especially on a one time basis, and interacting on an ongoing basis with a person who is "in your life" in some way—a family member, a friend, a spouse or life partner, or another ongoing significant other primary relationship partner. The basic characteristics of the latter sort of relationship (the significant other relationship) are its ongoing nature, its familiarity, and likely its relative degree of predictability, and perhaps even its inherent or expected loyalty to itself. (Note that some ongoing, even life long, relationships with a high degree of predictability are quite positive relationships that are good for both members, and others are highly predictable in their ongoing difficulties, problems, painful passages, and so on. See chapters 13, 14, and 15.)

To some extent, ongoing companionship with someone becomes a piece of one's identity—the self extends to include this relationship in its definition of its environment, or of its reality, and even of its self. Ongoing companionship, although frequently shifting to a stable state, an almost unvarying stable state, perhaps even a seemingly monotonous state, can mean security and safety, and yet also can mean stimulation in the sense that it provides at least some degree of ongoing interaction. It is this ongoing interaction, as the years go by, that can for many be THE lifeline, the adherence to this life, that many need "to keep going" (as more than one *Will You Still Need Me?* interviewee, especially among the older interviewees, describes this). What it takes to keep going as one ages is surely many things, however companionship is central much of the time.

This is not to question the fact that many older persons happily live alone and even find this a rich experience, because this is true (as we do hear from at least one older interviewee later in this book). This is to say that many other older persons who live alone do *not* find this a rich experience and over time find the number of interactions per week or month or year diminishing and receding. Engagement in the world can slip away. Slowly, almost undetected at first, like sand through an hour glass, connection to life may fade.

This trend in one's life can be quite slow and subtle. We may not see ourselves withdrawing from the world, little by little, especially where every step away from the world is but a very minor one. One fewer telephone call, one fewer birthday party, one fewer dinner with a friend, one fewer social event may not be noticed as these are but one fewer each time they do not take place. Still, over time a trend may be being established, and some movement away from the world, more and more movement away over time, may be taking place.

This is where a companion can be of great value, With aging, some decrease in desire for a wide "social audience" may be natural and even useful, as wide social audiences require and even demand precious energy, energy that we may need for ourselves as our energy grows somewhat more scarce. In light of this, a close personal companion is a naturally built-in social audience, one that may not be as demanding as a wider social audience or a larger social group (one that may be more rewarding at this stage of life by comparison to a larger social audience).

It appears that most young adults think about how they want to be sure to grow old, or at least older, with a primary personal companion, likely a significant other or spouse. They say that they want to find someone now, to grow old with later. This is more than just the breeding, family-forming to raise children, impulse. Somehow, this instinct to want a companion to grow old with appears to be built in, and does indeed go to work for us when we are young adults and looking ahead. And somehow, we may also just happen to sense that forming a new close personal relationship is easier at younger adult ages and becomes more challenging for many older persons. ("So why not do it while we can," one interviewee asked.) What the young adult may not realize is that close personal, especially intimate partner, relationships formed in young adulthood may not last through the years in light of the ever increasing life span, and the ever growing divorce rate, (and even in light of the modern mobility, transience, of all people whether married or not), which we see today. Or perhaps young adults realize this, as evidence of this is all around us, and this makes the prospect of aging all the more challenging and the desire to postpone looking aging fully in the face all the more strong.

II

BEING ALONE BEFORE
BEING OLDER

One of the signs of passing youth is the birth of a sense of fellowship with other human beings as we take our place among them.

—Virginia Woolf

In the Quiet of Time Passing. Photo courtesy of Angela Browne-Miller Collection.

Esmirelda Y., Age 38

Esmirelda Y. is a 38-year-old woman. Esmirelda Y. is married, has been for six years, and has no children. Esmirelda Y. says she has not thought about "aging itself much, but instead about getting worse." By getting worse, Esmirelda Y. is referring to her diagnosis of multiple sclerosis. Esmirelda Y. reports that at this time, she is weak, and her "disability is somewhat intermittent with periods of difficulty walking, and periods of extreme weakness, and then other times when I am better."

But the fact that her condition seems to fluctuate is not particularly reassuring for Esmirelda Y. She worries "that it will all get worse and worse, and that someday I will be very bad. Who will want me then? Who will need me then? Already my husband is telling me he is not sure he wants to take care of me if I get worse. This makes me think my marriage is temporary, that I can not count on it. I'm so young to be thinking about having the problems of old people—not being wanted, not being able to take care of myself....Hope all that is not on the agenda for me."

Esmirelda Y. talks about feeling, in her words, "very fearful and insecure about aging, because every day I am a day older, I have survived another day, but this is another day that may be closer to me getting worse and worse....I really wonder if I will want to live if I get real bad. I know people who have this real bad, and I do not want to be like that." Esmirelda Y. adds, "I think being old and sick is a double whammy, nothing very inviting, not a party." Looking ahead, Esmirelda Y. says, "What keeps me going is prayer. It is good that I have religion. I need it to go on, and to look ahead at my future. I have to believe in hope. I am not sure why hope is important, I am not sure how it works, but I know I need it to hang on to."

Patricia V., Age 45

Patricia V. is a 45-year-old married female. She and her husband recently welcomed their first child. Patricia V. is the vice president of a small insurance company, and "pushed back starting a family" so she could focus on her career. Sometimes this situation makes her "feel old. It's because all the other moms are so much younger. I think about getting older because I know that my husband and I will be in our late 60s, actually approaching our 70s, when our child is graduating college. And the 70s seem so old to me." While the 40s and 50s and even 60s don't really "seem old" to Patricia V., being a parent to a young adult, "say a 25-year-old" when she will be 70 now seems to be a concern for her. "I really never thought about it, not in a serious way, until after this baby was actually born! How strange is that?"

There are positive aspects of aging for Patricia V. She says that her career is now flourishing "after years of working toward this place" and she can now "enjoy all the hard work I put in when I was younger—to get to where I am now. I can also now enjoy the added perks of more time off, and, being in my 40s with a young child, I sure need it. I notice I get tired more rapidly now. That's a problem."

Patricia V. has never been divorced. "I was in a long-term relationship in my late 20s to early 30s, but it ended because it took a back seat to my career. I used to worry all the time that I'd end up old and alone, until I found my husband and he had the same aspirations as I did." Since

Patricia V.'s baby is only 6 months old, she says that "my child taking care of me in the future is the farthest thing from my mind right now. I cannot think about this right now. And I really would not like to think I will be a burden to my child. Anyway, my kid will be pretty young when I'm getting old, a young adult maybe, but too young to be taking care of old parents."

Although she now has a husband, she says that "Even before I married, the thought of being alone as I aged was never a problem for me. I always wanted a husband and kids, but I knew I'd be ok by myself if I got older and never had that. I think it's because I am, ultimately, a career woman. Until this child came, only my career mattered. Even now, I don't know what I'd do without my career."

"Right now, the only times I think about my friends aging is when I see how their age pertains to their kids. Most of their kids are 10 years or more older than mine. Does that mean they'll have more time with their kids than I will with mine? I do think about this, and am a bit uneasy, but I am more in the moment than all that, so I do not stress about it too much. This is just how my life has gone, I tell myself, and this is as OK as any other way of doing things. At least this is what I keep telling myself. But I love my baby very much and really wouldn't change a thing. I am so grateful that I was finally able to get pregnant. You know, these days women a lot older than I am, much later into middle age, are wanting to have babies...."

Devin P., Age 39

Devin P. is a 39-year-old married male with three children. Devin P. works as a senior manager in a technical job. Devin P. likes the idea of getting older because he thinks it gives him "more power in my religious community and at work. I don't think I'll consider myself an old guy until I'm in my 70s." Devin P. says he doesn't "give much thought to aging." He adds, "I take one day at a time. I don't think about getting older, not really." Devin P. says he expects his children not to take care of him when he is older, because he expects "them to be focused on their own children by that time. That is what I will want them to be doing. They shouldn't have to take care of me, or worry about me. I should be able to take care of myself. That is what I believe parents should do, or at least try to do."

Devin P. says "I don't worry about being alone when I get older. We got married in our early 20s, and divorce is not an option for us. I won't be alone, so I don't have to worry about it." Devin P. emphasizes that he doesn't "take aging that seriously, or really think about it that often. I don't really worry about my health. I know my future is good so my family is ok." Devin P. says that his "strong income helps me battle troubles in the economy" and that he "looks forward to retiring."

Devin P. adds that "turning 40 soon doesn't really bug me, not at all. I just want to make sure my family is ok. My wife says 40 is a big deal for her, that 40 is deep into middle age, but I don't really see why she's thinking 40 is getting old. It is strange for me not to care about getting older and for my wife to care. It's like we live on two different planes sometimes. She says someday I will care and then I will understand. But I say it seems we are getting older at different speeds. What's up with that? How is this going to be as we get older? I mean, I think married people are supposed to get older at the same rate. Right? What are we going to do if she ages a lot faster than I do?"

Story #11

Greg T., Age 44

Greg T. is a 44-year-old married male who is the father of three. He has two young children with his current wife, and a teenager from a previous marriage. Greg T. owns his own advertising firm. Greg T. doesn't like "the thought of getting older." Being 50 in six years isn't something I'm particularly excited about." With "parents heading into their 80s," he says "I've recently seen my folks age significantly. I'd say that being in your 80s officially means you're old." Greg T. doesn't want to get older because he is very active and has always had an active lifestyle. "A recent sports injury really scared me. I wondered if I would have had this kind of injury 10 years ago, or if it would have taken me as long to recover. Also, the pain seems to be harder to take when you are older. Gaad, that means I am older."

Greg T. has been divorced once. He says it "didn't have an effect on my thoughts about growing older. Maybe, in retrospect, it ended because we both had changed so much as we got older, so we were no longer compatible." Greg T. expects his children to take care of him and his wife when they're older. "We take care of them in the beginning, they take care of us in the end. That's how these things work. That's a given, and we've always told our kids that." Greg T. says that he cares for his own parents by "hiring people to cook meals for them and clean their house, to take the strain off. They'd never pay for those services for themselves, and I am able to help, so I do."

Greg T. says he fears being alone when he is old. "I don't want to be 65 and retired and sitting alone in this house all by myself. "He says all his friends have similar feelings about aging, and he's already lost one friend to a disease. "I hope my group of guys can stick around for a long time, and we can all be playing poker together in our 70s."

Story #12

Barbara H., Age 38

Barbara H. is a single female, 38-years-old, who has one child. Barbara H. had this child in her late teens. So she is one of the few of her friends who are about her age who has a child well into college. Barbara H. lives alone, and works in jewelry sales. Barbara H. says she doesn't "think about getting older a lot because it depresses me. I feel old already. I remember thinking that 40 was so old. Now I'm only two years away from that." Barbara H. is concerned about getting older "for a lot of reasons. For one, it's harder to date the older you get. Also, I live by myself and probably never will get married, so I wonder when taking care of my home is going to start to be difficult because of my age. Not yet of course. I climb ladders, fix things, and do everything myself."

Barbara H. says, "I don't think there are many positive aspects to getting older. The only nice part is that I can see how great my child has grown up." Barbara H. was never married to the father of her child, and found it "hard to balance being a single mom, having a job, and finding a man." Therefore, she explains, she never "managed to have a long-term relationship, although now I really miss having one. A husband would be nice to have as I get older, as I go though these coming years."

Barbara H. hopes that "my kid will appreciate all the sacrifices I made to be a good mom, and so take care of me when I'm old. But who knows. What if it's not an option for financial reasons or even because we don't live close enough." Barbara H. has never had to care for a parent or grand-parent, and suspects "it is demanding."

Barbara H. says, "I have already come to terms with the fact that I'll be alone as I get older. I've always been alone, and I'm used to it now." She adds that when she thinks about her friends aging she "sometimes feels lucky, because my kid is older and I have more freedom. It will take my friends until they're much older than I am to have the freedom I have now."

Barbara H. wishes that she had "made more money when I was younger to prepare for being older. I don't think I'll be able to retire until I'm in my 70s because I'm not rich and I have spent everything I have earned as I have earned it. Since I'll be poor when I'm old, I won't be able to afford to hire people to take care of me if I need it. This frightens me a bit. I try not to wonder what my old age will be like. But in the mean time, I have to ask what man would need or want me when I have so little to offer. I mean, I like myself, I really do. I'm not down on myself or anything. But I have to get real. I'm just a bucket of problems for anyone who wants a relationship at this point."

Story #13

Emily W., Age 47

Emily W. is a 47-year-old "single" female who lives with her "single" boy-friend of three years who is 30. (They describe themselves as "single but in love.") She has never had any children and doesn't wish to. She has never been married. Emily W. works in "media production." Emily W. likes her work, and is proud to have her work-life. She says she hopes "to work for many many more years....Retirement means I'm old. I'm not old, so I don't need to retire. I'll keep working until I can't any more. In my field, there is no real retirement age, thank goodness."

Emily W. does not like to think about getting older. "I don't think I'm old, my boyfriend doesn't think I'm old, so I'm not, right?" Emily W. says that "50 doesn't worry me. I don't think old happens until 70 or maybe 80, I don't know." Emily W. says her biggest concern about aging is the 17 year age difference she has with her boyfriend. "When I'm old, like, 70, he'll be 53. That might be a problem." However, she says they've agreed to "share our lives" and therefore she says she believes she "doesn't have to worry about being alone" when she "gets old."

Emily W. assists in the care of her 80-year-old mother, who lives in an assisted living community. Because she "decided a long time ago not to have kids," she says she doesn't know who will take care of her when she is "old like my mom." Emily W. says that she sees her friends "aging differ-ently because they have the strain of children, and I don't. I seem younger than other women my age and I think that's why. I think it's a choice: you either have some of your children to take care of you, or at least care about you, when you are old, or you stay young longer. You don't get both. I'll take staying young longer. Hope that works."

Story #14

Jeff B., Age 45

Jeff B. is a 45-year-old married male, who is the father of a toddler. Jeff B. is the director of a division at a business consulting firm. He says that "when I think about getting older, I get happy in a lot of ways because I like myself better now than I did 15 years ago. I think I've gotten better with age, like wine." Jeff B. says that he thinks his father "only now is old, and he's in his 80s now, so I won't be old until I'm 80 or older than that." Jeff B.'s biggest concerns about getting older are "getting Alzheimer's, which runs in my family." His father "started to show very slight signs of it in his early 60s, which is only 15 years away for me now. I have a toddler, I don't want to forget my kid when he's so young. But my dad only now at 80 got worse."

Jeff B. has never been divorced but says, "sure, I had some break ups of longer relationships before I was with my wife. But that's how you find a wife, you break up with everyone else. It wasn't because I was getting older that I settled down. Not really. Well, maybe it was a bit why, but not really so much. I love my wife, sure do."

Jeff B. assumes his "kid" will take care of him when he "gets old...because," he says, "I plan to leave him with enough money that he will be able to put some of it toward taking care of me if I need to be taken care of." Jeff B. currently pays for all the medical bills relating to his father's Alzheimer's condition and also will soon begin paying for the nursing home his father will be living in so he can have the 24-hour care he requires in his condition.

Jeff B. says that the possibility of being alone as he gets older worries him because "I always wonder if my dad would have been better if my mom was still around. Maybe he wouldn't have had such a hard time with his disease, or maybe she could've taken care of him." But Jeff B. feels that his family life is in tact, and that he has what he needs "to keep going and stay well. . . . Anyway, here's what I think I have figured out about getting old: I have a little child, so I have to stay young a lot longer than a guy my age whose kids are older. I'm banking on this."

Commentary

This second set of interviewee stories include people whose ages range from 38 to 47. We see, as the general ages of interviewees we review here creeps up, is older, a growing and more in depth awareness of age and of aging. Concerns about being alone when older continue from the first set of stories, however the intensity of these concerns appears to be increasing with age. Some of these interviewees, such as Esmirelda in Story 8, are even contemplating what it might be like to be left or abandoned by the person believed to be (or once believed to be) one's life partner—and to be left or abandoned in midlife, early midlife in her case.

Most of these interviewees are deep into the family building, child rearing, and or work/career building phases of their lives. Aging is out there, however not yet knocking on the door. Still, there is a deep unsettled undercurrent of question regarding the future. It is out there: the future is coming, aging is coming.

The future, aging day by day, is something out of our control. And yet we live day by day, dealing with the host of significant and pressing present time issues, as these are front and center at this time: raising children, marriage issues, divorce, sandwich generation, empty nest, work life, finances, and unemployment issues—all these and more are holding the attention of these and this study's other interviewees in this age range, at this time in their lives.

Somewhere in here, the notion that midlife has arrived, or is at least knocking on our door, comes over us. Entering midlife is itself a great adventure, or better stated a great challenge. Midlife, once we notice we have entered it, is also a wakeup call: Time does go by, we do get older day by day, year by year, decade by decade. Not only does midlife signal the arrival of full on adulthood (for those who have not yet realized they are right in the midst of adulthood), but it also signals the receding of youth, and the eventual approach of older age, then old age, and then old old age.

6

Midlife Looks at Aging

Midlife, that wide amorphous span of time between young adulthood and older adulthood, begins and ends at different times for different people. It might also be said that midlife is getting longer. We are not sure exactly when we enter midlife, we do not say, "hey, let's have a party for her, she just entered midlife." However, we do enter midlife when our young adulthoods come to a close. Furthermore, these days, the old do get older later. For some, midlife appears to be reaching even into the late 60s and early 70s and will soon (perhaps for some) even reach into the mid 70s.

Does this mean midlife will be extended to include not only the 30s, 40s, and 50s, but also the 60s and 70s? Midlife is at least in part the product of the length of the life span. We might say, as the life span extends, midlife extends as well. Midlife is also the product of the definition of retirement age—of the average retirement age. As expected retirement age extends to a later and later age, midlife extends with it.

And for many, this extension of midlife is a welcome development. It is part of the new "forever young" perspective. Where once, we cherished being 20 forever, now we cherish being 40 forever, even 50, and someday 60 forever. In fact, we are pleased when we hear that 59 is the new 39, whether or not we truly believe this. As this shift in thinking takes place, the median age of one's "settling down" (or whatever that means to those who talk about doing it), is taking place later and later. And with this later settling down age that some people exhibit, there is the accompanying later childbearing and the accompanying extending of the childrearing age span. (Note that trends are working in opposing directions in this regard: Many younger women say they want to be "certain to have children young enough to enjoy them," while others want to establish their "marriages, careers, and financial lives" before having children.) In fact, the desire to have children later in life, into one's 30s and 40s, is quite common.

Other trends extending midlife are also making themselves apparent now. Many of these trends are in the domain of expectations and demands placed upon us (by others and by ourselves). Among the extenders of midlife demands is the great new extender of childrearing years: *adult child rearing of one's own adult children*—a newer occupation in our modern times. Children, even well into adulthood, appear to be remaining dependent or somewhat dependent on their parents for longer, at least financially, and frequently socially and emotionally as well. Some parents even face parenting demands well into their 70s and 80s, some of these demands wanted, some not. (While such demands may not be entirely or even somewhat undesirable in many instances, there are situations that are past the limits of normalcy or of mental health. However, even normalcy and acceptable states of mental health are something to be determined by each family.) Some parents may like, and even perhaps feel they need, this situation, this adulthood caring for adult children. They quite frequently even encourage this, or at least inadvertently support this. The issue becomes one of what is best for all concerned, and of being able to clearly determine what is best for all concerned. Helping one's children to prepare for adulthood, and for the independence required for most healthy adulthoods, is central in parenting. (Helping one's children at times during their adulthood is not unusual. Helping one's adult children avoid adulthood is something else all together.)

There are significant modern changes and shifts in: the expected ages for the birth of one's first child and then the birth of one's last child; the time these children (their generations now being born over a longer period of time) live at home; the time these children remain at home as they enter adulthood; and the degree to which they remain dependent upon their parents, especially financially, well into adulthood.

These days, one's adulthood-age span (to leave out teenage parents here) of child rearing, child raising, child supporting, can reach from approximately 18 to approximately 70, with the age upper limit of 70 now being modified, fortified, and even extended in various ways. For example, there are many options open to "older" parents or those who wish to be older parents these days—such as fertility drugs (for those who wish to help their chances of getting pregnant), surrogate pregnancies (for those who are willing to carry a child through its birth for someone else, more and more these days for money), and adoptions (for those who will take a child in and make it part of their own family). These options make it more and more possible to have a baby at a later age where one's body may say no. Adding to these parenting opportunities are those ever more common legal arrangements such as custodial parent-grandparent agreements and or court orders. All this means that the 18 years of raising the child can begin later and end later in the parent's life.

All this makes it possible to be parenting one's children not only into one's 40s, but also into one's 50s and even 60s and 70s—perhaps even beyond. And we simply can no longer say that when the parenting of children under 18 ends, midlife ends. And we can not say that the only or primary parameter of midlife is the range of childbearing and childrearing years. Clearly, other parameters do exist as well. These include the time when one retires (as noted above), the time when one is expected to leave the workforce (whether or not one does stop working), the time when one becomes a grandparent, and of course the time when one feels OLD, truly old.

Feeling old is a complex sensation. There is the physical component—what moves less freely, what aches, what looks old, what looks physically older, what part of the body does not work well, what does not work at all anymore. And there is an emotional component—what feelings go with feeling older, feeling one looks older, feeling as if one looks quite old, feeling as if one is being treated as being old, and perhaps most importantly, feeling as if one is no longer needed.

7

Divorce and Being Alone

The family forms a boundary around itself, defines itself as a distinguishable entity, something recognized by outsiders as having boundaries. These boundaries may be permeable, even gentle boundaries, or they may be well defined and perhaps protective, or they may even be rigid and unbending. The family boundary or protective cage is generally a good thing—it defines and therefore actually makes possible, creates, and protects families.

Nothing rattles the family cage quite the way divorce does. Divorce is the rearranging—the redefinition, the break up, and sometimes even the shattering—of the family boundary or cage. The family's boundaries are broken when one or more of its members pull or are pulled (or are pushed) away full or part time, breaking through the boundaries, to form new boundaries—even new identities—around their new social, emotional, and physical realities or locations. Following many divorces, the previous form of a family is pretty much gone, the new family or families that emerge after divorce form their own new cages with their own new boundaries, and to do this, need the old cage to release them (at least in part) from their old identities. Many of these new family forms include just one newly lone adult, an adult who now serves as a single head of household, a single parent, or a single person living entirely alone.

Of course, alone can be a good thing. Yet, too often, the postdivorce aloneness can be discomforting, perhaps somewhat challenging, and for some, even harrowing. Regardless of one's age and state of mind at the time of a divorce, the cracking of the family cage can be ungrounding, disorienting, confusing, distressing, even shocking for some. Among the effects of divorce are the leaps into stages of aging that are usually (where they do occur) chronologically later in life. Divorce can take years away from one's life, as divorce is one of life's major stressors. Divorce ages people, everyone, in some way, some more than others. In essence, divorce propels some people into experiences more typical of older persons: loneliness, depression, agitation, helplessness, and brings with it the health effects that do come with both loss-grief and social isolation experiences (as described in chapters 17 and 18).

As the ages of divorces are now extending into people's 70s and even 80s, we see the profound (although not always negative) impact of divorce magnified by age. It is in this time that the question of the hour can shout out from deep inside us: *Will anyone still need me?*

8

Welcome to the Delicious Sandwich Generation Years

Never enough can be said regarding the unparalleled experience of being sandwiched between two or more generations. Being needed (if "needed" is the word here—we could say "wanted" or maybe even "pulled upon" as easily) concurrently by both one's (child age, teen age, college age, and adult age) children (and sometimes grandchildren as well) and one's older parents (and sometimes grandparents as well) can be almost too much. After all, if you are going through this phase of life, you may be feeling a significant degree of stress, wear and tear, and even depression. The multiple care giving roles of the sandwich can descend upon us when we least expect them, when we least need them, when we least can actually perform them—and yet somehow we do or at least we try.

While history tells us that traditionally the woman and mother who had been the stay at home mother to the children would naturally assume the role of caregiver of the parents and parents-in-law, history also tells us that times have changed. For one thing, the majority of women, mothers and middle age familial caregivers now work outside the home. Care giving traditions are changing or diversifying rapidly. For another thing, generations are growing farther apart in years, and grandparents are significantly older than they were in earlier years, which means the grandparent form of familial caregivers are likely older as well.

The physical, emotional, and even financial demands placed upon the sandwich generation are growing and augmenting, while the relief for middle age sandwich generation caregivers is no where in sight. One's own plans for the preservation of one's own health, one's own professional development, or simply one's own ability to hold a job, one's own retirement plans, and so much more, are frequently shelved out of love and necessity. Once we are free again to look after our professional, financial, retirement, physical health, and emotional lives, we may be no longer able to give ourselves what we may deserve or simply what we need. Retirement saving, physical stamina, professional opportunity, emotional fortitude, and more may be all spent and even irreplaceable. Is the wear and tear upon us here to stay? Do things get better? Are there rewards that balance these out?

These are not easy questions. Rather than bringing with them definitive answers, things we can be sure of, realities we can expect and count on, these questions present great unbudging unknowns. These are the unknowns that form a great and looming sense of uncertainty in aging, one many persons never manage to shake as they grow older. Uncertainty itself is a state of mind, a psychological condition, one that deserves our attention.

9

⸺∞⸺

Worklife, Career Loss, and Not Feeling Needed

"I'm a 63-year-old man. I worked for a corporation for 40 years. I was laid off when it reorganized. And now I can't find a job. No one will hire me. I guess my skills are outdated. I guess I am outdated. But I need a job. I really do. I keep applying and getting turned down. I've applied for hundreds of jobs. This is bad. I feel useless. It's like I don't exist anymore. Not having work and not doing what I have been doing my whole adult life makes me feel like I am dying or something. No one wants me. No one needs me anymore."

If you are 50 or over, look behind you. You see an army of adults younger than you are, seeking the same jobs you are seeking. They have updated skills and likely more energy than you do. If you are 50 or over you are likely to be watching younger generations follow you into, and then take over, some of your professions such as reporting, teaching, technical work, computer programming, and more.

Even if you are not looking at this development (or even if you feel you do not need to be looking) you may sense the pressure, and the competition, at least subconsciously. And you may feel the subtle but potent conflict here. The survival pressures affecting the younger generations rub up against the survival pressures affecting the older generations. Step over the line, age a bit, put on a few years, and you are now the enemy—at least on some level. Sure, the younger generation includes your children and grandchildren or future grandchildren. Sure, if they are competing for your jobs, moving in on your place in the workforce, you can be proud you have instilled the work ethic into them and thereby into the next generations. However, now this same work ethic stands up and seeks to bump you from your own place in the workforce.

"Darned if you do and darned if you don't," one 58-year-old parent and grandparent says. "First, you want to be sure your kids don't grow up lazy. You want to be sure you won't have to support them forever, because it's not good for them and then because you really can't afford to. But then, they and their friends or peer group turn right around and want your job. But if they take your job away from you, they won't be able to support you because it's the same as you not making enough money on this job to support them."

So here we are again, in the double bind, the face-off between generations, generations who love each other dearly—and you do want each other to survive, yes? Is there anything we know deep down inside ourselves, anything that tells us something otherwise? We might want to consider an evolutionary psychology perspective here.

Evolutionary psychology is a field that explains psychological traits as adaptations that evolved in response to conditions that existed in the environments of our ancestors. Of note here is the fact that in ancestral times, grandparents, parents, and children were closer in age than they are today. It is only in modern times that the distance between generations has increased. Still, the drives that emerged long ago exist within us. As a result we still tend to make decisions that relate to our best survival or perceived survival outcomes. We do what it takes to increase the chances of our survival in all instances.

Yet, what our survival is may not be entirely clear to us—on a conscious level. We may not see what is driving us. Our survival is not just our own personal survival, but also the survival of our offspring who will carry on the family line. Therefore, we make decisions based on what is most likely to fuel and ensure the survival of our offspring, putting our children first, sometimes even before ourselves. In fact most of us have seen someone or ones give their adult children money until they themselves are penniless.

Why does this happen? Do the people who do this realize what they are doing? Frequently no. Instinct, the drive to ensure the survival of the family line (the offspring) even over the survival of the self (the parent or parents) where these two are in conflict, can kick in and guide behavior— even when this behavior harms the self (parent or parents). This same behavior, the drive of some parents to do everything and anything they can to feel that they are ensuring the survival of their offspring, can run awry.

What, this instinct can turn against us—have the opposite effect? Wait, what does this mean we ask, how can this be? First let's take a look at this instinct. Yes, this is instinct, we are indeed wired this way. This instinct is likely as old and time tested as the human and even many other (if not every) animal species are. And this is good. While children are young (from birth to 18 or so), most parents typically respond to their internal wiring to take care of these young people who are dependent upon them. They are ensuring that these children make it through childhood to adulthood and then are no longer dependent—so that they will eventually be able to raise (and support) the next generation as it grows from birth to age 18 or so.

When adult children still need us, we feel the tug of that instinct. It is after all our job to ensure the survival of our offspring. Yet when we support or form the basic support for adult children, we must look carefully at what we are doing. We may be assisting these children in getting started in the adult world. We may be helping to pay for a college degree for example, or helping the offspring to acquire some other form of job training. We may be a good fallback in case of emergencies. This is great, of course, and makes sense.

Yet we may also be encouraging (without our realizing in most instances) financial and emotional dependence at a time when we would best assist by encouraging independence in our adult offspring. So while we drain our own financial, emotional, and energetic resources helping, we may be taking away from, discouraging, the much-needed independence we actually should be encouraging in our adult children. Encouraging independence can be a valuable contribution to the survival of our offspring and its ability to bring in and help make strong the next generation—and to teach that next generation (your grandchildren) how to encourage its offspring to be strong and independent as adults so they pass on to their children the same survival skills.

Now let's return to this whole matter of workforce participation as we age, as this relates to the above discussion as well as the one in chapter 9. This is one of the emerging human rights frontiers. We might want to say the obvious here: We have a right to remain in the workforce as long as we can participate in the workforce. We should not be faced with forced retirement, or a set retirement age, or penalties if we do not retire—should we not retire. Do we have as much right to participate in the workforce as do our offspring—as does our generation's offspring and its offspring? This would be the case for what is described as workforce equality (treating everyone of every age as someone who can compete for a job) and the case against age discrimination (denying people over a certain age equal opportunity when applying for jobs).

Lets look at age discrimination for a moment. Age discrimination, although as troubling as other forms of discrimination, is frequently excused by arguments (whether or not reasonable) against hiring older persons. Arguments excusing age discrimination may include: hey—older people are not equal to younger people; the training and skills of these older persons are outdated; these older persons do not learn new skills as rapidly; it costs too much to retrain these older persons while these younger persons arrived in the workforce with these skills or with nothing blocking them from rapidly learning these skills; we have to pay older persons too much, as their salary histories are long and have been climbing over the years, while these younger people come in and can start at the bottom; or, we are able to pay younger persons higher salaries, greater benefits, because they are better investments and the training we provide will pay off in far greater ways.

Arguments against age discrimination may include moral and ethical reasons for placing as much value on older members of the workforce as we do on younger. These arguments may also include: older persons bring experience to their work, although difficult to measure is essential to work quality and productivity; older persons deserve a place in the workforce as they have built what we see out there today; older persons should be honored with places in the workforce as they are our elders; social security is already not enough for many retired persons to live on, and therefore these persons deserve the opportunity to remain in the workforce.

So on a larger generation to generation scale, when older persons move over for younger persons, they are helping to ensure the survival of the next generation. But we may want to ask: are they placing their own survival second to the survival of their offspring? Are they doing this because they are being driven by that deep wiring, the instinct to help ensure the survival of the species, via the next generation? Do social regulations and employer behaviors reflect this wiring?

All this comes back to the question of the hour: *will you still need me?* And if you will not still need me, not still need me in your workforce, for example, *why?* Is it that we are wired to need older persons less and less as they age? Is this an absolute—that we are needed less and less during the last decades of our lives? Or can this absolute be modified, changed, revised. Can we indeed rewrite the path of aging, and the place for aging, in our world? I say yes, and we must begin with our own perspectives on aging, to reach others people's perspectives. The whole new paradigm I refer to in the preface of this book must emerge and demand center stage.

10

⚬⚬⚬⚬

Empty Nests

Eventually finding oneself somewhere in the stage of life commonly called "middle aged" has emerged as almost a given. And this stage of life is viewed as growing ever longer. Where once what we may think of as midlife was at best 15 years long—from 35 or so to 50 something, now midlife can extend on and on, until one wants to relinquish the title "middle aged" or at least the phase midlife itself. If we look at history, we find that life expectancies were generally short enough that midlife was maybe all of life until being old at the age of 40 if you were able to live that long.

As life spans extend, the upper ceiling on average life expectancy raises. This means that what was once considered old is now increasingly considered midlife. Where once midlife began at 30 or 35 at the latest and ended around 45, midlife then shifted to the time period from about 40 to 60 and then to the time period from about 45 to 65. And now midlife itself is pressing the perceived limit and raising the midlife bar to more like 45 to 70. Today, at least in many modernized post-technological revolution cultures such as that in the United States, midlife does begin whenever someone wants to admit it has begun and does stretch until 65 or 70 or maybe even 75.

The "middle aged" people who were interviewed for this study tend to think of themselves as caught in a somewhat uneasy limbo, and many express a sense of tension between the drive for their own security as they age and the drive for the security of their offspring. (See again the previ-ous chapter.) How can this unlikely tension, riddled with wrenching di-lemma, arise, we wonder. How can we find ourselves here, in this moment when we feel we must choose between our children and ourselves?

One woman, married and in her mid 50s, describes this tension as "a trap that you cannot escape. You see, you care about your kids, you are proud of them, and happy they grew up so well. But they are young adults and working to make their way in the world. So when they come and need some money from me, I cannot say no. But lately, every time I give money to one of my kids, I feel that I am taking it away from myself. And even though my kids say they will pay me back, I know it will be a very long time, if ever, that they can."

Another parent of adult children, this a divorced man in his 60s, sees this tension differently. "I worked all my life to have what I have today. Why should I share this with my daughters? They can work to get it for themselves. I do not give them anything, not anymore. I told them long ago, I would send them to college and then they were on their own, and I meant it. They are not always very happy about this, and they say I am selfish. But I think this makes them strong. And it keeps me from worry-ing about my own money and my own older age too much."

Where one's own sense of security is pulling in a direction opposite of one's own sense of her or his children's security, confusion arises. After all, we are programmed to ensure the survival and even viability of our off-spring. How can it be that we feel we have to deny them what they need or what they think they need sometimes, especially as they get older—and as we get older? "How can it be that the terrible feeling can get worse once our kids have kids, because it does," one interviewee asks.

Whether young adults actually feel more safe and secure than do the people their parents' age (or than do their parents) is unclear. Especially when parents are under pressure or unemployed or underemployed, or in some other way unable or not able to be the safety net they were for their children when they were growing up, then young adults may experience as much or a parallel insecurity to that of their parents.

The entire question, *will you still need me?* becomes more one of *will WE still need who and why will we still need them?* Need is such a vague word, at least as per its many uses and abuses. While the basic definition of "need" is about as vague as the use of the word, we understand the word "need" to mean (a) that something is required or "needed," and that (b) some-thing which is "needed" is essential in some way, and that (c) that state of not having enough of something essential to survival is the state of being "in need." Frequently, the word "need" is converted into an expression of desire, as in "I need you" or in Spanish the quite common "Yo te queiro" (I want you, which means I need you for all intents and purposes).

Need itself, as a spoken word, and as an experience, as well as a perception, is stretched to include or at least to blur with want. Certainly, certain need and even dire need can be accompanied by certain and even dire want—and vice versa. However, as economists have long emphasized in their study of consumer behavior, needing and wanting are two different things. Yet these are confused much of the time. In the end however, you can want what you really do need, or you can need something but not want it. Yet you can only think you need what you want but do not really need—you just can't want something a lot and have this want turn into need just because you think it should. We all know the phrase lovers exchange: "I need you, come back to me, I will die without you."

Children and their parents may or may not use these words, want and need, interchangeably all the time, however these two words are blurred both in usage and in thinking. It is difficult to want something very badly without believing one is in great need of it.

And then there is the not wanted and the not needed side of the story. One version is experienced by one lover falling out of love with the other lover. The wanting and perceived needing of that person who is no longer loved is over, or at least reduced. Another version is the sensation some parents feel when their children, now being young adults, leave home. Mom and Dad, or Mom or Dad where the parents are single parents, are just not needed anymore, or not very much anymore. The "empty nester" is the no longer needed parent left alone in the nest where the children were raised. Sitting in an empty nest is very difficult for some parents. The sensation of feeling no longer needed rings with a sort of "your life is over" bell. After all, the life as it was, the life where the parent was charged with seeing to the survival of the offspring all the way through to adulthood—that life is over. Empty nesting is not experienced by all parents whose children grow up and leave home, however for those who do experience a severe case of empty nesting, their identities, their routines, the way they find meaning in their lives, their reason for getting up in the morning, most of the patterns they have established—can be shattered and leave in the wake of their wreckage emotional shock, emptiness, turmoil or even despair.

The ability to be resilient when family life circumstances change radically is a powerful determinant of the quality of one's survival into older age. This does not say that survival in terms of health and longevity is ensured by empty nester resiliency, yet it does say that emotional survival, emotional balance, is fueled by resiliency as offspring leave home.

Understanding that all that was, all the routines—and ways of living, being, and working, were built around protecting the offspring and seeing them into adulthood—are no longer needed is a big step toward moving past the empty nest syndrome. How readily we can get caught in this gulf between phases of our lives, and just linger there. How readily we can stay stuck in the space between phases—where just yesterday most everything we did was for the well-being and even survival of our children, and today most everything we do must be for our own well-being and survival—or for our just making it through another day alone.

Interestingly, more parents are feeling not only the strain of providing financial and social and even emotional assistance to their children for years (normally virtually two decades from birth to age 18), and for years and years (where some adult children never leave home or leave and "move back in again" or leave but stay emotionally and or financially dependent upon their parents). As they feel these unexpected strains, more and more parents are relieved when their children finally leave home and finally take care of themselves. (Parents ask themselves and blame themselves— "What have I done wrong that my child is remaining so very dependent into adulthood? It has to be my fault, yes?")

So parents tend to feel both touches of empty nest syndrome and waves of relief that their children are actually growing up and taking care of themselves. However the price we pay for liberation from offsprings' dependence upon us may be balanced with the price we pay for being alone, lonely without them, and living in an empty nest or place.

Past middle age into older and old age is another need-want experience. Now those who need may not feel needed in return. As one 75 year old interviewee explains, "I want to be needed, but I know I am not. I want not to need my family very much, but secretly I need them more than I ever have. I want a lot of things, such as wanting to be needed. But most of all I want not to need too much, and not to need to be needed too much. That way it won't be so painful, this not feeling needed...."

What is the pain of aging? It is really out there? Yes, many will answer. Yet this pain is elusive, almost difficult to document. It waits in the shadows—the shadows of our subconsciousness, and works its wiles from that angle. This invisible but all too present pain is frequently denied, suppressed, ignored, or simply blocked from our awarenesses. We just don't see the pain or want to see it. "It's too scary to think about being very very old and very very alone. I just can't even imagine what it's like. I certainly never want to find out," explains a 62-year-old woman, a divorcee who was interviewed for this project.

There are other perspectives on all this. An 80-year-old male, a widower who was also interviewed for this project says, "I expect that my family will come and get me someday and then put me into one of those homes. I'm going to fight that. I'd rather die than be put out to pasture like that. Thank God, right now, and I hope forever, I'm fine on my own....Life just isn't fair. You take care of everyone for years, work like a maniac day after day for decades, for your whole life practically, and then you finally are free to do what you want to do for yourself, and then they think you can't take care of yourself so they want to lock you up....It's not fair. They all needed me once, and now all I need from them is my freedom. I don't need them and I don't want to be needed by them and I don't want them to need to put me in a home."

The tension inherent in many people's aging processes is sometimes muted and is sometimes shouting itself full force right into our ears—if we are listening, that is. There is anger, yes, and there is also fear and pain regarding aging itself and regarding everyone around the aging process and regarding one's own inability to stop the clock. Many of those interviewed for this book who are in their 50s, 60s, 70s, and 80s express these feelings either directly or by referring to these feelings, as if keeping them at arm's length so as not to experience the whole full on. Yet this mélange of emotion and of numbing to emotion is out there, it's in the atmosphere, looming around us, in our faces but hidden to many until they actually have to deal with it, aging, themselves.

It's not that we haven't been informed that aging is coming, and that aging can be tough, its that we want to avoid admitting this to ourselves, we want to protect ourselves from this thing out there as long as we can. It's the elephant in the room...a mean one at that.

Of course, not all aging is a negative experience, and we should resist painting it that way. In fact, many of those interviewed for *Will You Still Need Me?* report that: "Aging has its benefits. You can look anyway you want, pretty much, so long as you don't let them think you are crazy that is." "No one expects you to look like a model anymore." "You can get out of doing things you don't want to do by being very sleepy, or messy, or achy—or just acting like you are not going to be any good to be around so they don't make you go do it." "I like acting strange at family events, so I can get out of them more often." "You aren't needed all the time, which is a relief...but you still want to be needed sometimes, you know."

III

---⚭---

SOCIAL PATTERNS, RELATIONSHIPS, AND AGING

Old age is the most unexpected of all the things that can happen to a man.

—Leon Trotsky

Holding My Place in Time. Photo courtesy of Angela Browne-Miller Collection.

Story #15

Peter S., Age 49

Peter S. is a 49-year-old married male. He is the father of two children, one of high school age and one of college age. Peter S. is a marketing director for a well-known corporation. Peter S. says he has "just recently started to think about getting older, but in a good way." He adds, "I'm looking forward to retiring and moving with my wife to wine country. Once both the kids are out of the house, we'll have the freedom to do that. Downsize our house and spend more time doing the things we love. I think we deserve that." Peter S. says that he sometimes thinks he's old, but doesn't really feel old. However, he does think that "anyone over 75 is actually, and for real, quite old."

Peter S. says one of his biggest concerns about getting older is not the possibility of his finding himself alone, but of his wife ending up alone. "I've always been the provider, she hasn't ever worked....Well, I mean she has taken care of the family but not worked out of the home. I take care of my wife, I do. I support this whole show, and I worry that my wife would not be able to do it if something happened to me. And, most of all, I don't want her to end up alone."

Looking ahead at "being old," Peter S. says that his children "had better take care of me and my wife. It's their obligation. They actually owe us for raising them and supporting them all these years. I mean, I do love them, but this does not mean that I don't care if they give back or not. I expect them to help me if I ever need it. And my wife too." And,

Peter S. is already doing the same for his mother-in-law. He currently cares for her (his wife's mother) who lives with them six months out of the year (the other six months she is with Peter S.'s sister-in-law).

In the past year, Peter S. lost a life long friend to a heart attack. "I was very scared, then very sad. I couldn't function for a little while. Then I remembered I was still alive and I wanted to stay alive. I really had to think that we're all getting older, and this was a little heavy for me to cope with. Aging is for real. And health matters. I just didn't want to think about it before now, not this way. So now, health is a concern of mine."

The economy is another of Peter S.'s aging concerns, as he "lost a lot of money when the economy tanked. Right now, it's all about fixing what happened to our finances so I can retire comfortably with my wife in wine country. I am focusing on our future now, while I am young enough to. This really doesn't leave me much time to think about anything else. I will for sure deal with my soul and God and all that later, I won't forget to, I know it, because these things are important to me. But right now, I figure I've got 15 years or so, (if it takes 15 to 20 years, then so be it), to make a lot of money and put a lot away. I think this is enough time to reach the level of savings I want to reach. When I'm secure, then I'll pray. I was raised praying so I know I can get into it again someday. Does this sound like I'm doing things in the wrong order?"

Story #16

Katy B., Age 45

Katy B. is a 45-year-old woman, who has been divorced for two years. She has two children who live with her half time. She says she is always very lonely when her children are with their father, her ex-husband. She adds, "It is unnatural, this shipping the kids back and forth between the two parents. The kids are never in one place for long enough to be settled. The parents, (well at least me, the mom), are always worrying about these kids—and always lonely. Always. Maybe this is what being old will be like, Lonely a lot. I guess I'd better get used to it now."

Katy B. reports that her concern about aging is that she could "get too old to marry again and actually really end up all alone." Katy B. works full time, and reports that "with the kids, and the job, I have no time for dating, no time to find someone to be with." Katy B. reports that she never thought much about aging until she was in the middle of a divorce, and "then I started worrying I would never marry again—and I have not married again so far. Things aren't looking good along those lines."

Katy B. notes that being 45 makes her "a little too old to find someone to marry again. Men are looking for younger women, not someone with this much baggage, not someone with a difficult ex-husband and two wild kids and all this hurt and all these wrinkles on my face. Plus I need a new career now. I have to find a way to make more money, so I also have to go back to school online or at night while doing all the rest of this. When

I finally have time to do something about my being alone, I'll be too old to be able to do it, and I will always be alone then."

Katy B. continues, "Some of my friends invite me to meet other people at social events. Some invite me to religious meetings. I always say no thanks, I don't have time. I really am too busy to socialize, it is true, but also, I don't relate to a lot of things my friends relate to, such as religion. This doesn't sound good for me, but I don't see anything I can do about it. The divorce has had a big impact on my state of mind. I'm discouraged and not hopeful. I don't feel good about myself, not anymore....I'm already old, and not pretty anymore. This divorce aged me 20 years. I'm really feeling like one of the old people, with the problems, or at least some of the problems, of old people....Maybe I shouldn't be feeling this way at 45, but I am. Maybe this is not being grateful that I still am younger than many older people, and more fortunate I am sure. I do feel guilty for feeling like this, but I do feel like this. I just can't make myself feel less lonely. Thank goodness my children need me. I need to be needed by someone."

Story #17

George L., Age 51

George L., 51, is, as he says, "a happily married man. We've been together 20 years, and we still love each other." George L. adds, "Well, I mean we didn't exactly get married, not according to the law, because you know this thing with same sex couples, all the discrimination against us. But you know, we did a ceremony of our own. And we are very committed. We may be an unusual couple, but we are a good one and a stable one. Lot's of married people don't have good or stable relationships but we do."

When asked whether he ever thinks about aging, George L. responds, "Not until recently, when I started feeling old. It happened all of a sudden it seems. My bones started aching and my energy diminished. Doctor says there is nothing wrong with me, it is just age. Age? I'm only 51! But I guess this means I am aging, whether I like it or not. It sure makes me think I am. And I'm not really happy about this."

George L. says that when he thinks about his future, he realizes he does not know what "it" will be like, that "my future is a giant unknown." He says that this not knowing what his future will be like is uncomfortable for him. He feels as if his older years are a "great big question. I don't know how I will get through them really. But at least I know I won't be alone, as I have someone I have been with most of my adult life. This is reassuring. This is my meaning in life, and my identity, and my security. And you know, I also have God. You see, I believe in God, and believe God is always with me."

When asked to say more about what he feels as per the aging process, George L. replies, "Well, you know, I would have preferred to never get old, to always be young and sharp and handsome, but if I have to, then I think my state of mind is a good one for aging. Also, as a same sex couple, as it gets called, we are more likely to be very stable if we have lasted this long. If we were not a stable couple, we would have broken up early on. Having someone to grow old with, someone who has known you for a long long time, makes aging easier, I think. I sure hope I'm right. I've got a lot of years ahead of me to find out if I'm right."

Mark R., Age 56

Mark R. is a 56-year-old man who lives with his "female lover" as he describes her, and two dogs. They have no children. Although Mark R. and his girlfriend are not married, Mark R. makes it clear that they are "as good as married." Mark R. says that as he grows older, he tries "not to think about aging very much," but that "new aches and pains do have me sort of worried about aging." Mark R. notes that he is "not really afraid of aging" but rather he describes aging as "a big hassle."

Mark R. had not given much thought to aging until his "friends' parents started dying" and now is "starting to think aging is a bigger deal than people say it is.... It's like this big awful thing looming out there, waiting for us. And we know we can't escape it.... But I also think that aging can be what we want it to be, I mean we can't stop getting older, but we can try to accept it and be OK with it all.... I mean, why fight it when we cannot fight it?"

Mark R. says he is not expecting to retire from his "day job" for another 10 or 15 years, and is concerned about how well he will be able to live once retired. Mark R. also notes that "I think I should have thought about having kids years ago, as kids are a good thing to have when you are old, so you won't be alone. Sounds unfeeling of me I guess, but that is what I think having kids is really all about. Most people won't tell you that, but it's the real truth isn't it?"

Mark R. went further into the notion of being alone: "I've never really been alone, never really wanted to be alone, and hope I never will be alone. I don't like being alone, not at all." When asked what being alone might be like, Mark R. replied, "Empty. Dark. Lonely. Painful. No one to say your name," and then began to sing under his breath. "I do keep music in my life. It feeds my soul. I need to feed my soul, not sure why I know this, but I am sure I do."

Story #19

Sally S., Age 52

Sally S. is a 52-year-old woman, divorced, living with her "manfriend" as she describes him, and their two cats. Her children are in college, except for the youngest one, who lives with the other parent, Sally S.'s former husband. Sally S. describes aging as "a long, difficult journey, or at least that's how it looks to me from where I am now, the age I am now.... But wait, am I old now, old already now?" Sally S. views aging as something that is "often sad and painful, and can be very lonely." Sally S. says she wonders whether, when she is old, anyone will care about her or for her. "This is a pretty terrible question to be asking myself. These are the sorts of things we all try not to think about before we have to."

"When I am older, my kids will be even more busy with their own lives, which they should be. My ex-husband, well, he could care less. And since this is confidential and you are changing my name, I can say that this man friend, my current beau, is not necessarily going to stick around as I get older. Basically, I think men are going for youth and looks in women, and will keep going for youth and looks as long as they can. It makes them think they are staying young. It makes me feel sort of useless, unwanted, disposable. So if I can't keep my looks, God knows what I will be facing."

Sally S. is concerned about being "old and poor and all alone, but I am not really working on trying to prevent that. I wouldn't know how to prevent that happening to me in the future anyway. Getting old just happens to you, that's that. You have no choice, so why think about it all the time.... Anyway, maybe things are getting better for older people now, with medicine and everything finding new ways to help older people, right? And at least there is Medicare. At least. Sally S. notes that most of her "women friends" are in their 50s and that they "are thinking pretty much the same as I am these days."

"I sure wish aging was something we all could be looking forward to, like a big reward after years of hard work. Shouldn't we all be rewarded for living and bringing children into the world? And for making it this far? But I don't see anyone handing out rewards. And I stopped believing in Santa and the tooth fairy a long time ago." When asked whether she has a spiritual, religious or other belief system and world view to guide her, Sally S. responds, "Do you mean God? I also stopped believing in God a long time ago. I really don't believe in anything except what is right before my eyes everyday."

Story #20

Sandra M., Age 55

Sandra M. is a 55-year-old woman who lives with who she describes as her "woman friend and significant other (or domestic partner)" who is 10 years younger, 45, and also with their 10-year-old child. Both Sandra M. and her domestic partner are employed full time. Sandra M. says that between the two of them, "we manage a middle class living and are relatively alright. But we do worry about retirement. Thank goodness it is a way off into the future. Yes?... Well, sort of way off. For me, it is closer I guess."

Sandra M. expresses some concerns about the fact that neither of them have any savings or investments toward retirement and that "life has been too demanding for this." Sandra M. reports that both she and her partner are in good health, and that this is what she describes as "helpful, reassuring, and probably too taken for granted."

Sandra M. also says that she expects she and her domestic partner will "stay together forever, even after our child grows up. However, you never know, and I do get worried about this because it does get harder to find a living companion as you get older. And I need a living companion. I don't do well alone. It would be awful for me to be old alone." Sandra M. expresses concerns about being alone "if something happens to us, if we break up, or if one of us has to move away for work." What might being alone be like for Sandra M. is a question Sandra M. says she tries not to ask herself. She does "not want to think too much about the possibility," and that "Just living day by day is hard enough without worrying about being old old.... I'll deal with that later." Sandra M. says she is "thinking pretty much the same way as everyone we know: Life is good, but challenging. The future, well we hope it will all work out. We have to hope because we feel we don't have much control over our future. Hope is pretty much all there is. Isn't that what everyone thinks these days?"

Sandra M. then describes "down days" she has once in a while when she just sits by her window all day, "trying to be happy and not get too depressed...." It is on those days that Sandra M. feels nervous, as if she is "sensing what the future will be like" for her. "But I have more happy days than down days so I keep going."

Geraldo H., Age 54

Geraldo H., 54 years old, is separated, and uncertain as to whether he and his wife will be divorcing or re-uniting. At this time, he lives alone, in an apartment, which is very near the family home where his wife and two teenage children live. Geraldo H. thinks of aging as "something to worry about later, when you have raised your kids and they are on their own. You really cannot age until then, I mean you cannot get old until then, because you are needed. You are needed, your time is needed, your attention is needed, your paycheck is needed, your hard work is needed, your patience is needed a lot, and you feel it. You feel pulled in all directions, but I guess that is being needed."

Geraldo H. wonders "what it will be like when the merry-go-round stops." He is concerned that he may experience a let down, something akin to what is described as the empty nest syndrome, once that merry-go-round stops. He says that it will be then that he will feel "lost, and old because the main part of my life will be over. . . . I won't know what to do with myself when no one needs me anymore. And I will be too old to start a family."

Geraldo H. feels that part of his separation from his wife is that they are "both looking ahead at what life will be like when the children have left home. We've been all about the children the whole time we've been married. I guess we aren't about anything else and never were." Geraldo H. is concerned that he and his wife will "have nothing at all to say to each other when we are not being full time parents anymore, and when we are not needed in this way anymore. Then it will be just us. Will we need each other then? I'm not so sure." He adds that sometimes he just wants to "run away from it all," that he does not want to face his "present pain" and certainly not his "future loneliness."

Commentary

Now, in these still more-to-the-point and straight-from-the-heart stories, are those stories of some of the interviewees whose ages range from 45 to 56. We see here in these stories that aging is taken ever more seriously. Here the stakes are still higher. Time keeps moving on and on now, and every step is another step closer to the older years. Time feels somewhat shorter now, although perception that aging is here is not quite front and center, clear—yet. It is as if aging is coming into focus.

Many of these interviewees have fully moved into actual or possible sandwich generation concerns. Many of these interviewees are dealing with family and partner concerns as well (marriage, divorce, new mates, no mates, etc.). Those who are without a life partner, or are unsure of the primary relationship that they do have, now feel that time is shorter and that finding someone to spend the rest of one's life with now may be more difficult than ever.

Also central among these stories are significant concerns regarding money, money now, and in the future. These interviewees are largely concerned about their own futures as they age. Many of these people do expect that their own children will be there for them as they age, if needed. However, there is a lingering doubt—what if there is no one, no mate, no child, no family member, no community, to care or to be able to care?

Aging within the family and within society—within the surrounding networks—is front and center here. Connection to these networks is felt to be (sensed as being) a virtual form of life support now and in the future for everyone at any age and for every one who is growing older. When these networks appear to be or actually are dissolving, or are at all shaky or being questioned in some way, the sense of the future is also dissolving, or is shaky or at least being questioned. We reach this part of midlife and we ask: Where are we now—and who will we be in the future—and is there really a future we want to move into?

We wonder who will be there for us as we grow older, and then quite old? Who can we count on? And, who can count on themselves to commit to be there for us and then make sure their commitments can be realized?

11

The Aging Self within
Surrounding Networks

The human being is an animal that forms small, medium, and large net-works—families, communities, and societies. Whole lifetimes are spent within, and or in and out of, these networks that encompass each other. One is born into, or connected in some way to, at birth or during child-hood, these networks. And, one ages into, or is connected in some way to, while living life and aging, these networks. The need to feel needed, to be wanted in some way, to fit into the surrounding social networks, is satisfied in large part by these very social networks of family, community, and society. Family needs you, community needs you, society needs you, all at certain points in your life. And you need them as well, perhaps more or differently, at certain points in your life.

But is there a moment in your life, do you reach a time, when neither family nor community nor society really *needs* you any more? If so, how do you survive this moment, how do you exist once this moment has arrived? What changes for you? What stays the same? We can see how families can protect at least some of us from this moment, or from the full impact of this moment. Many families cherish the grandparents, even value their help with children, with decision making, and with other parts of life. Many families actually support the grandparents. And many actually pro-vide either indirect or direct hands on care for the grandparents.

Families are very important to us, especially in a survival-oriented way, at the beginning of life, when we are very young and naturally dependent upon our parents for survival. And families can become important to us in some of the very same survival-oriented ways again in the later phases of our lives—if we still have families, and or still have access to families, and or still have families who can spend time with us or provide for us in some way anymore—or still have families who need or want us, that is. (This is not to say that families are not important to us at other times in life, during other phases of adulthood. This is to say that we are most likely to depend upon our families for our own survival most at the beginning and quite frequently also at the end of our lives.)

The aging process includes the aging of *our relationships to the networks* in and surrounding our lives. To varying degrees, we are dependent upon our social networks at all times in our lives. We move through levels of total dependence as babies, through levels of lessening dependence and growing independence as children and teens, through levels of independence as adults, into levels of changing forms of independence as we move through adulthood and age—and then in many instances back through levels of dependence in older age. Every step of the way, these dependence-independence processes tend to be played out in well-established patterns. Aging itself is part of the overall life cycle pattern. Try as we may want to, we are always living within this major, overarching super-pattern: be born, grow up, grow on, grow older, grow old, grow very old, and eventually pass on. And being able to live all the way through this life cycle, this super pattern, from beginning to end is a great gift (as we see when people are not able to live through their life spans as a result of malnutrition, illness, injury due to accident, interpersonal/personal violence, crime, or war.)

Moving through the life cycle is truly a magnificent albeit challenging experience. Ultimately, every person must either ignore, or react negatively to, or better, manage to come to terms with, growing older (come to terms on a personal level—internally, psychologically, even spiritually—whatever spiritually may mean to the individual). Sometimes aging is denied, or thinking about it is avoided, and sometimes aging is surrendered to as if losing a war, or instead aging is fought, or feared, or resented. These responses to aging—denial, avoidance, surrender, fighting, fearing, and resenting, can work their way into the general state of mind. It is not surprising that we may find many older persons appearing to be in states of denial, avoidance, surrender, fight, fear, and or resentment (whether they are in these states—or only appear to us to be in these states as we tend to assume or project that this is what is being experienced). Sometimes the life cycle (super-pattern) does feel confining, a sort of trap, in that there is a predetermined aging process that will take place—if we are fortunate enough to live long enough to undergo aging, that is.

You cannot stop the clock. You cannot stop getting one year older every year you live. The confines of this life cycle super-pattern taking us from birth through the end of life are real. Some people do indeed fight these confines and yet others live through the life cycle with acceptance. Some of this acceptance is a blind acceptance, an "it is what it is" feeling, as one interviewee for this study described it. Others arrive at a very personal, often private, quite sublime acceptance—not only making peace with the aging process, and the reality of the life cycle, but also finding that adjusting to aging is actually a deepening experience. Some people actually find aging to offer them an awakening of the spirit, the emerging of a strong sense of being part of all creation and of thereby belonging to nature's greater process, nature's overarching cycles. For the most part, aging is something that happens to us as we live. It's a given. We can look for the positives to help cope with any negatives, so some of the interviewees in this study say. Yes, we can find these positives, we can even generate them deep within our hearts. (Please refer to the Cycles within Cycles figure in Part Seven.)

12

⸎

Families, Patterns, Networks, and Aging

Families tend to be at the core of other social networks that, in turn, almost all tend to encompass or involve families in some way. This is largely because most people are born into families, and they begin their lives and likely end their lives as family members. Deep within the family system, at the core of many families, is a partnering relationship, frequently a love relationship. This partnering relationship is, in many cases, what initiates the formation of that family in the first place—by partnering and then, in many instances, by bringing children to this partnership—thereby further forming the family. Note however that families do take varying forms including: the more traditional two parent families with children; and also couples who have no children, and other single parent, two parent, multiple parent, and stepparent combinations, grandparents as parents, and still other teams. Note that single people who may live alone do in their own ways form single person family units (although of course themselves also coming from families of their origin and also being part of these families they were born into—as is everyone else a part of the family of origin).

Whether they be families in their various forms, or communities, or societies, or some other form of human organization-communication-perpetuation, all social networks are based on patterns—patterns in present time, and patterns emerging over time and carrying themselves forward in time through the social networks that are transmitting these patterns.

For example, a behavior pattern found in a family today may be much the same as a behavior pattern its ancestor families also exhibited. Generation after generation, family and community and social patterns are transmitted into the future. Yes, the patterns are adapted to accommodate the current environment, and yes, these patterns do evolve. However, these patterns are, by their very nature, patterned to preserve themselves or to change only incrementally over time—so as not to rock their boats so to speak.

Of course, boats do get rocked. Even within patterns that work to stay the same, these patterns can be rocky and threaten themselves from within (or call in threats from outside). And some patterns are even patterns of rockiness—up and down and up and down and up, anger and makeup and anger and makeup and anger, and so on. At the most basic level, where family patterns are brought together by two people who form a love and or an intimate partner relationship, positive patterns can be maintained, or less than comfortable and even negative patterns can emerge and also be maintained. In essence, these patterns (whether positive or neutral or negative patterns) that define these relationships are *needed* to define and even preserve these relationships. Again, these relationships are found at the core of many larger societal patterns. (Note that patterns "want" to live on, just about as much as do people.)

Interactions between people are central in these networks made of patterns. The patterns we see in intimate partner relationships are for the most part interaction fueled. (Keep in mind that an interaction may be a spoken one, a silent one, a physical one, an economic one, a withdrawal from interaction one, and so on.) All this interacting is social; all this interacting is the social behavior humans are known for. Again, every single interaction and even seeming noninteraction we have with each other is a sort of social interaction. And again, social patterns underlie most every interaction. So this is all quite intertwined. We actually need this intertwined system of interactions, patterns, and networks to exist within social systems—to survive there, and to live to grow older and then live old there.

What does this mean to intimate partner relationships over time, and into midlife and into older age? Does this intertwining continue as people age? Or does this intertwining weaken the way aging memories and aging muscles sometimes weaken? Do interpersonal interactions and the patterns they take place within, and the social networks they hold together—fade away? If and when these functions start to fade for us as we age, are we sending ourselves a message—or might we feel we are hearing a message from the world around us—that we are no longer needed to hold the fabric of society together? Or the fabric of community? Or the fabric of the family? On some level, we—our minds, hearts, and bodies—are always asking these big questions: *Will you still need me, world? Will you still need me, society? Will you still need me, community? Will you still need me, family? Will you still need me, significant other, intimate partner, life partner, spouse? Will anyone still need me?*

How do we navigate our aging processes in light of these hidden (and yet not so silent) questions? Do we tell anyone that we are asking such questions? Do we even tell ourselves? We may not realize we are wondering such things. We may not be privy to this running dialog taking place deep within our subconsciouses. Still, we and the course of our lives, are profoundly affected by this ongoing and ever growing wondering, by this major life question regarding whether we are needed less and less as we age.

Like still water, such a question runs deep.

13

Intimate Partner Relationship
Patterning and Aging

Let's look deeper for a moment and see the intimate partner relationship or relationships that are at the hub of much of society—and also are a big piece of many people's life spans. The intimate partner relationship is an intricate, wondrous system of processes and functions between people who come together largely by way of two highly rewarding and reinforcing processes: one—various forms of attraction; and two—social norm (social expectation) fulfillment. This is a good thing: people come together to couple to form intimate partner relationships—and then frequently do bring children into the world and raise these children and thereby keep the human species going. But what does this relationship mean to us as we age? Does it stay the same or adapt? Does it last or hollow or fall apart?

So we know we are biologically and genetically programmed to form such a relationship or something like it to serve the perpetuation of our species. We are even biologically programmed to try to hold that relationship together to raise the children born out of, or coming into, that relationship—or to find another way to be a family unit for those offspring if that original family breaks up. Many times this coupling, which may have first occurred to bring in children and then raise them, holds itself together as is, or reforms itself to hold itself together, while the members of the couple age. And a long-term relationship holding itself together as its members age can be a good thing. Stability and a sense of shared history in one's life as one enters mid and then older age can be quite a healthy and positive experience. (Although this may not be the only positive path through aging.)

However, not all coupling partnerships are healthy and positive experiences. Sadly, a sizeable subset of the population of intimate partner relationships is that of troubled intimate partner relationships, which are too frequently undetected—or not admitted via denial functions, or simply accepted as "normal," or worse, simply ignored. In the domain of the troubled intimate partner relationship reside habitual detrimental attractions, and various abuses and violences ranging from emotional to economic to physical abuses and violences. This situation remains quite relevant as members of the couple age.

Troubled relationship patterns can live on as people age. Even where the expression of patterns of troubled behavior weaken with age, these patterns themselves can have become deeply ingrained, virtually a part of the self and the identity. Even where these patterns and their effects may be less and less outwardly visible as people age, these patterns may not be, and often are not going to be, gone. Some people live with the scars of previous or ongoing troubled relationship patterns, and or of previous or present self-harming patterns (which sometimes include staying in troubled relationships) for the rest of their lives.

While many primary partner "marriage" type relationships appear to "mellow" with age, this apparent mellowing must be recognized as something that can indicate a positive development or something that can indicate other than a positive development. One or more situations may be occurring: a true mellowing or softening of the situation, perhaps an actual healing of the troubled relationship, or a problematic adaptation to the troubled patterning and the feelings that accompany it. The latter is not desirable, as it is an adaptation to and an acceptance of, even a perpetuation of, the troubled patterning, which can be dangerous for the mental and physical health of all involved, no matter what the ages of the partners.

Many relationship patterns (within one long-term relationship or while moving from relationship to relationship) are formed at stages of life when people's love and sex hormones flow quite freely. It is important to keep this in mind when we think about aging relationships and about aging within relationships. Many relationship patterns are profoundly habit forming. Attraction itself is a good example. A note here. Habitual attraction itself, founded upon interpersonal attraction and overarching social norm, is not in itself problematic, and may in fact be some of the "glue" that keeps well-functioning couples and families together. While eventually the relationship can become almost a habit, even well into older age, this can be good habit. It is when this function runs awry that patterns of troubles, risks, and dangers can emerge and then remain over the years. Furthermore, there is something that keeps even these troubled patterns that have run so far awry in place, helps these patterns that, like all patterns, want to survive. This something is this same characteristic of a pattern, even a troubled pattern, to perpetuate itself, to keep itself going on and on: this is the characteristic addictive nature of any self-perpetuating pattern. So love and relationship patterns and behaviors developed earlier in adulthood can stay with us the rest of our lives, (or can at least shadow us the rest of our lives).

Again, many positive patterns can be addictive; addiction to a pattern may be quite natural and positive where this is a healthy thing. Even being in love is itself an addictive experience. Even without the running awry found in a troubled relationship pattern, a healthy love (and or sexual) relationship can parallel a drug "high" especially in its early stages. In fact, love is in essence a drug that activates the brain chemistry in a way that resembles the brain chemistry occurring in persons who are taking neuro-stimulating drugs such as cocaine. There is even a high or addictive rush when people are falling in love, are in the early stage of forming attachment patterns. This high is so very rewarding and reinforcing, which once experienced, one does not want to lose that feeling, and experiences great distress if that feeling is removed much the way a drug addicted person experiences a withdrawal when that drug is removed. We are driven therefore, even programmed therefore, to try to keep that love relationship together even long after the original love that brought it together has faded—even if possible into old age. And if that basic primary love relationship does not last, does not make it through midlife and well into older age, we are without what is for many a major life-sustaining component of our lives. What an irony it is that some of the primary reasons for sustaining a positive primary partner relationship into old age—to stay connected with one's history, and to continue having the companionship provided by this long-term partner in our lives as we age and move on into and through old age—are also some of the primary reasons that some troubled relationships continue on into old age: history and companionship. The positive health effects of companionship in aging are clear (refer again to chapter 12). However the negative effects of a troubled relationship pattern are also clear (as per this chapter and also chapters 14 and 15).

In midlife, if a primary relationship falls apart, we may be driven to seek a replacement for the relationship, to reform that lifelong pattern that was so powerful for us, powerful enough for some of us to form a family unit out of it. In later life, this drive to replace the missing member of the long-term intimate partner relationship takes on a new dimension. Now we are even further from the stage of life where hormones and emotions are programmed to drive us to form partnerships out of which families are frequently born. Now other factors take hold. For some, being a member of a relationship is the *only way of life* they know. If they lose their partner, they are somewhat—or in some cases seriously—lost, almost without half their identity, or without what feels to be all of their identity.

Now, the search for, and the actual reinstatement of, this or another replacement "love" sensation is more difficult, not being fueled by those old hormones, and is not always an option. For many, when circumstances such as divorce, disease, or death compromise or end the primary relationship the life long identity is compromised. The state of social isolation so common among the elderly can even begin in midlife and can even be magnified. Basic engagement in interactions recedes and basic membership in some social patterns dwindles. It is as if a piece of the self drops away and all that social patterning that has been so much a part of one's lifelong existence is being suspended—a bit out of reach or perhaps entirely out of reach. Stripped down of the social networks—or of participation in the social networks—one knows and has been part of for so many years, midlife and older age without a partner can be quite a rough journey (at least for some).

But not for all. Some older persons actually say they "prefer to go it alone," or to "finally find" themselves, to "go inward." And many persons actually find that as they enter later middle age, and post middle age, and older age, they desire fewer, or have energy for fewer, social contacts. (Note that this does not mean no social contacts, it means fewer and actually fewer contacts at once.) Many also notice that they prefer smaller social gatherings to larger ones, and more one on one time with a close friend or family member than more time with many people or with people they are less close to. (We return to this matter in chapters 16, 17, and 18.)

14

Patterns of Behavior
that Continue

As we grow older, we carry within us lifelong patterns of behavior that continue to influence us. Our patterning, our programming, runs deep, even deep as still waters. We are influenced by both inherited patterning, and by patterns of responses we have learned just the day before and also at earlier stages of our lives. We have a library of experiences that influence our present time behavior, and this library is both our genetic and our learned memory. Out of this library comes direction, coding to do this or that when confronted with this or that. We don't always see the direction to do what ever we are doing coming at us, welling up from deep within; yet, the direction can still be there.

And, it is from deep within that impulse arises, or better said, that impulse strikes. Strikes is more to the point here, as impulse is rapid onset behavior that occurs without time to think about what is taking place. Of course impulse and the reflexes it controls are essential to survival. For example, we are coded to get out of the way of danger as rapidly as we can, or to stand up and fight that danger right away, without stopping to think. This is the all important fight or flight reflex. However, this fight or flight reflex can slow down, become less responsive, less reflexive, less impulsive, as we age.

Much of our behavior is driven by impulse, at least when we are young enough to have rapid onset impulsive responses. As we age, our impulses and reflexes may slow a bit, or may wear down. Our impulse responses grow not only somewhat slower, but are also perhaps less precise. We just may not leap as quickly. Or as accurately.

So the power and speed of some impulse responses fade somewhat as we age. Nevertheless, our patternings and memories are driving us even when we do not realize they are. Old memories last longer, strangely are more durable than newer short-term memories. Sometimes as we age, fresh memories sitting in our short-term memory banks are not as secure as long-term memories. Some but not all aging people find that these short-term memories can be rather transient; they may not be stored as well. Many of these memories just may not work their way into the long-term memory bank as short-term memory grows less and less efficient—unless purposefully exercised to remain efficient. (Note that not all aging people experience great amounts of this memory inefficiency.)

So as we age, we can be overpowered by what our long-term memories tell us, whether or not we see this happening. Many of our responses to our own long-term memories (when triggered by present reminders) are themselves buried so deeply we do not see them at work right away. We may respond—in the now—to what our buried memories of past responses are responding to. We do this rapidly, as rapidly as is typical for us at our ages (whatever these are at the time), until we have time to think—to reason with ourselves—to see what is happening in the now. Of course by the time we see what our reaction is reacting to, we may have already reacted and be (what I chose to call here) *neuropsychologically invested* in the process. Once invested in the reaction, we are somewhat if not fully committed to it.

Deeply buried long term memory has, in a sense, been socialized (and even sometimes traumatized) to the point where it reacts to present day events as if these were harbingers of past events. Past comfort may seem to be present comfort; past safety may seem to be present safety; past danger may seem to be present danger; past pain may seem to be present pain. For example, take a person who has been hit in the face many times as a child, and who long ago grew to cower and fear these repeated assaults. Many years later, in adulthood, there is nothing like this in that person's life. One day a friend reaches to adjust the cap on that person's head and that person flinches and raises a fist, almost hitting the hat-adjusting friend. Had the person not been so rapidly placed on automatic by the buried memory, then she or he could have warded off (or changed in some way) her or his behavior in the now.

There is a difference in the speed at which we respond to things triggering a rapid onset impulse response and those triggering a well thought out conscious response: the conscious response is slower than the impulse response. We access memories that trigger impulse more rapidly (at least in terms of milliseconds, which matter in brain time, however may not be observable on a watch) than more conscious memories, although we don't see this in the moment. The effect of this difference in speed of access to deeply buried *impulse-driving memory* and to speed of access to conscious *thinking-through-response-memory* is powerful, as both memory pools are being accessed almost (in real world—every day—time) simultaneously. I will call this the *reaction differential factor,* or RDF. As we age, the RDF grows smaller and smaller: there is less difference between rapid onset impulse reaction time and conscious purposeful reaction time. At the same time, impulse reflexes may slow and weaken, bringing down the RDF still further as we age. Time passes. We grow older. The time we take to respond to a stimulus slows. The long-term memories may never the less be driving our behaviors.

15

Hollowing to Patterns

We spend lifetimes burning social, emotional, and behavioral patterns into ourselves, and then reinforcing these patterns again and again. We even addict ourselves to both our positive and our negative patterns, as we are genetically coded or wired to do this. We addict ourselves to the ups and downs of these patterns, the on's and off's, the highs and lows of these patterns. We clearly are riding these patterns through our lives—until the obvious parts of these patterns begin to wear down, or our expression of these patterns grows softer, quieter, less expressive. This is not to say that the emotions that are felt as we ride these patterns fade with age. On the contrary, these emotions, even if they grow quieter or less obvious, may be felt quite deeply. All too often, a much older person is seen as having a less emotional response to something quite disturbing when actually this response may be greater but less overtly expressed.

As we live, we grow used to the many basic emotional patterns we may identify with on deep levels. Examples of these patterns include:

- longing for, craving, the sense of contact with someone or something— then finding relief from craving contact, and contact with something or someone in some form;
- longing for stimulation—then finding relief of longing for stimulation in some form—such as interesting conversation, or excitement(e.g., its adrenalin rush, etc.);

- longing for, craving, relief from discomfort—then finding relief from discomfort in some form.

And...

- tension building—then finding relief from tension building in some form—perhaps by relaxation or sports or television or sex or drugs, and so forth;
- pain building—then finding relief from pain building in some form—by taking pain pills, or sleep, hot and cold compresses, and so forth.

These are common and frequently overlapping emotional and physical longings and patterns. We have all experienced some of these. When these patterns are experienced repeatedly over time, we can begin to submerge ourselves in these patterns—we can begin to identify with these patterns—*to even confuse ourselves for these patterns*. Left unaddressed, untreated where help to leave such patterns is needed, this identity with long-term emotional patterns does not just disappear as we age. These patterns do not just go away. They may not remain as visible, but they may be more deeply buried. Always remember, still water can run quite deep. So can loneliness and longing. So can sadness, hurt, and pain. We must keep this in mind when we talk about the emotional patterns of an aging person. What we see on the surface, what is expressed outwardly, is not all that is there.

Some patterns are locked into some relationships for so long that the relationships become these patterns, virtually nothing but these patterns. Note again, among the patterns we see develop in people's lives are patterns of trouble in troubled intimate partner relationships. (Of course these are not the only patterns, and of course not all patterns are negative or detrimental.) Some people spend their entire adulthoods living in troubled and even abusive relationships. Here again we see an addiction (albeit perhaps a quite unwilling and unconscious addiction) to a pattern of emotional highs and lows; and, we know that such an addiction can have distinctly detrimental effects. Prolonged addiction to roller coaster rides of stress or even of abuse and violence increases the probability of more and more damage and more and more severe instances of damage and injury over time. This sort of addiction can be built around the sorts of longings and cravings listed earlier (e.g., longing for stimulation, longing for contact, longing for relief from discomfort, and also tension building and pain building cycles).

Somewhere along the line, sometimes even from the very start (in early and mid life adulthood) when attraction and or love is intensely biochemical, we may cross check points on a path that could be traveling from: general interaction, to attraction, to emotional issues, to emotional abuse or habitual nonphysical abuse, to habitual physical violence, to addiction to the highs and lows of the pattern of relationship abuse and violence itself. This is not to say that all or even a majority of relationships follow this path, although far too many relationships do. This is to emphasize that everyone in a past, present, or future relationship, especially a long-term relationship, can benefit by knowing about these paths, warning signs, and checkpoints. To say that anyone who has or had a relationship should not look at this issue is to say we support denial of this issue. To never have looked as we grow older while in a relationship is especially risky.

The matter of patterns becoming us, or of us becoming patterns, is especially important as we grow older. Patterns, burned in over time, can grow increasingly deep and increasingly rigid. Sometimes people experiencing patterns of long-term ongoing relationship disappointments and troubles—whether these be emotional or physical or other—can appear to others or even to themselves to grow numb to the emotional and physical pain. This is not to say that now no emotional or physical pain is felt. Not at all. This is to say that there can be a growing layer between the self and the anguish the self feels itself feel, a growing layer between the self and the anguish the self knows it is feeling.

This *numbing to pain* takes place because the ongoing emotional and or physical pain can be too much to bear on a fully conscious level. This numbing to pain can also be the result of developed tolerance. This numbing behavior, whether a tolerance for pain or a coping skill of some other sort, is terribly dangerous. This numbing renders all involved, especially the person or persons in pain, capable of missing protective, even life-saving cues. They may not see how serious the situation is, and or may not feel the intensity of the pain—even while in great distress (being abused, or even being maimed, or nearly being killed, or being killed). Contrary to programmed safety instincts, (such as pain aversion and pain avoidance), safety is compromised by the numbing to the very pain that would allow the sensing of the true level of danger.

This process can take place in any abusive relationship at any age. However, at older ages impulse and response times may be slower, and emotional and even physical pain may register more silently and more internally. At older ages, signs of abuse and its related pain and anguish may register less visibly for the individual being abused as well as for outsiders who tend to react to what the individual being abused reports or shows signs of. Older people may not track their experiences and sufferings entirely consciously, or as responsively. The pain and anguish nevertheless registers quite deeply within the person being abused. This is the scenario in which we can have *abuse of older persons without detection by the self or others*. Again, still waters run deep, and they can be the still waters of deep but silent sufferings whether or not these fully register.

This development is the surrender of a basic survival instinct to what is in this instance an acquired maladapted survival instinct: tolerance to pain (and abuse). As some persons age, while many of their conscious sensations may be becoming less intense, and many of their obvious responses to these sensations may be receding; what appears to be, or may actually be, dangerous numbing to and tolerance of pain and danger can actually be increasing. Again, this is not to say the emotional pain is gone, this is to say the emotional pain is registering perhaps more silently, perhaps, though, ever more deeply.

What tolerance can look like in troubled aging relationships (with intimate partners or even with family members of another sort, or even with nonfamilial caregivers) is a numbing to the experience of being abused (as well as to the experience of abusing where this is also taking place). Again, we must remember that numbing to pain, or to abuse and even violence, does not prevent the emotional and physical damage it causes, rather it can allow it. And it can allow it to grow worse, because the fear and pain avoidance functions are slower, as are all impulse responses.

Especially in watching for caregiver, intimate partner, or family member abuse of the elderly, note that while the intensity of suffering may increase, the apparent (to outsiders) sensation of "receiving" the suffering may appear to decrease over time. This is not to say that the suffering itself is less, not at all. The suffering is taking place whether or not it is recognized. It is easy to wrongly assume that if there is no apparent physical abuse there is no physical abuse. It is easy to wrongly assume that if there is no apparent emotional abuse there is no emotional abuse. Many older persons suffer in silence for the rest of their lives.

It is also easy to wrongly think that if there is no physical abuse, there is no emotional abuse. Hence a special comment regarding emotional abuse here. Long-term patterns of emotional abuse, especially of the elderly, are quite common. Of course, emotional abuse can be elusive. Patterns of emotional abuse are underway all around us, affecting almost everyone of us, at least in a minor form, at some time in our lives. Emotional abuse patterns are so very common that they are too often taken for granted, as normal and acceptable. Emotional abuse tends to take a back seat to physical abuse as physical abuse is seen as more damaging, more dangerous, and more specific. In fact, many persons who are being abused emotionally but not physically do not recognize this abuse as there is not a distinct physical sign of it, although the scars can run quite deep. And of those being abused physically, many do not include emotional abuse in their descriptions of the abuse they are experiencing. Still, the effects of emotional abuse can indeed be just as powerful as the effects of physical abuse.

It is important to see that even adults (as is true of children) experiencing emotional abuse may not see that this is taking place. Feelings of discomfort such as these listed here may not be attributed to emotional abuse, even in instances of high levels of emotional abuse. (And of course, the feelings listed below are not definitive indicators that there is definitely emotional abuse.) However, these are quite common responses to emotional abuse, especially to abuse of older people:

embarrassment

confusion

instability

identity doubts, not feeling like oneself

worthlessness, low self-esteem

no or low level of confidence

sense of complete or extreme failure

depression

isolation

no sense of control over what happens

all-encompassing self-blame for every problem

humiliation

pessimism, a negative outlook on the future

And eventually, persons being emotionally abused by someone over long periods of time can add to this list:

feeling that the criticisms of oneself being made by someone are correct, believing them

defending these criticisms to others or even to oneself

believing these criticisms of oneself

And sadly, sometimes these self-abusing behaviors arise:

> joining in silently or verbally on the emotional abuse of oneself
>
> hurting oneself emotionally or physically
>
> amplifying the abuse being experienced by working to hurt oneself even more than the abuser does
>
> hiding the pain in substance abuse or other detrimental habitual behavior
>
> severe depression
>
> possible tendencies to suicidality, suicidal tendencies

Sadly, it is quite common yet quite understandable that people can endure exposure to a negative experience better when this negative experience is part of an ongoing pattern. Being part of a pattern we have grown used to, we are less shocked by the negative experience. (This does not mean we are also less traumatized or injured by it.) This increasing endurance of long patterns of abuse takes place not only on individual, but also on family, community, and societal levels. We are a social system that too frequently ignores, denies, looks away, from elder abuse—whether it is elders' abuse of each other in some long-term intimate partner relationships, or abuse of elders by others not in such relationships (some family members, some caregivers). It is truly as if society does not want to really know, to know the pain and horror of what is taking place. More of us need to acknowledge that this is taking place and to speak up about even the subtlest and most invisible forms of this abuse—even when we are urged not to speak about this, and not to see it.

Rocking the boat rocks the boat. And the tendency is to avoid shaking things up, to preserve the status quo, good or bad, whatever this may be. Lies keep the boat from rocking, yes, until the boat springs a leak, or sinks, and one or more of its passengers drown.

IV

---✁✁✁---

AGING ON AGING

How pleasant is the day when we give up striving to be young—or slender.

—William James

Being Older Together. Photo courtesy of U.S. Administration on Aging, via PINGNEWS.

Story #22

Marcia G., Age 64

Marcia G. is a 64-year-old woman who lives alone. She is divorced now for 10 years, is not in touch with her ex-husband (although he does regularly send court ordered spousal support checks), and has two grown children. Both her parents are deceased. She has no siblings. Marcia G. describes herself as "pretty much alone. My sons live on the other side of the country, are very caught up in their own lives, and I have no family out here. In fact, my sons are my only family." When asked how she feels about this situation, she says she "is more and more afraid there will be no one if I really need someone."

Marcia G. is also concerned that were she finally able to move closer to her sons (by moving to the "other side of the country"), she would discover that they not only do not need her, but also do not want her "around much." Marcia G. thinks that "having the entire country between us is a godsend, because I don't have to deal with the pain of being rejected." She says she has never discussed the matter with her sons, and really does not know whether they are rejecting her or just "busy living their lives." Marcia G. adds that she does not want her sons to worry about her, that she can take care of herself, and that she should take care of herself. She also adds that the alimony she is receiving will continue the rest of her life, or the rest of her husband's life. "It's not much, I have to work to add to it just to pay my bills, but at least it's a help. But, I don't know when I can retire, because the social security I will get will not be enough, and if something happens to my ex (husband), then I'm not going to have that added help."

Marcia G. decides to add, "I never expected things would end up like this. If I could go back and do things differently, I would have stayed with my husband and not divorced him, even though he hit me a lot, even though some of my friends had said they were worried he was going to hurt me badly or kill me one day.... These days I think having a bad marriage might be better than being so lonely and insecure at my age.... I remember meeting a woman who saw how upset I was after being beaten by him. She said to me, make it work, don't leave him, or he will end up with the house and everything you own, just because you walked out. Deal with the hitting.... At the time I thought she was wrong, and now I wonder. At the time I was not thinking about being 64 and so alone."

Story #23

Linda B., Age 62

Linda B. is a 62-year-old married female. She and her husband have never had any children. Linda B. was married once before, in her 20s. Her then husband died in a car accident. She was a school teacher for 25 years before she recently retired. Linda B. says she doesn't think much about getting older. "The past couple of years since my retirement have been filled with a lot of travel and a lot of fun, so there hasn't been much time to think about aging." Linda B. adds, "We've been retired for a few years now. It means we have freedom to travel and enjoy our lives the way we always wanted to."

Linda B. thinks that 80 and older is old, and "sometimes I get surprised when I realize how close 80 actually is, it's only 18 years away....I don't feel like I should be that close to being OLD. It's even more surprising when I realize it's only 15 years away for my husband." Linda B. says her greatest concerns about getting older are health related. "I worry about arthritis and the impact it will have on us being able to move well and travel easily."

Linda B. and her husband have no children, and therefore, she says, they have "no one to take care of us when we get older." Linda B. notes that they "do own several properties and are hoping that these investments in real estate will financially support us if and when we need some sort of help or assisted living....Later, much much later, I hope," Linda B. adds. "Gosh, I'm not ready for all that."

Linda B. adds that "I wish having children had been a higher priority for us. I could have adopted if I really couldn't get pregnant. I think the two of us liked having our lives and our two incomes all to ourselves and so didn't have children. Maybe we were selfish. Maybe not having kids was a big mistake, I don't know."

Story #24

Tom M., Age 56

Tom M. is a 56-year-old married male. Tom M. has three adult children. He owns his own small law firm, and his "business is thriving more than ever." Tom M. notes that he isn't "too keen on getting older. Your mind slows a bit. . . . And, no one WANTS to be old," he adds. Tom M.'s parents are in their late 80s, and Tom M. thinks they are "the epitome of old to me. They look old, they act old. They're old. I don't want to be old like they are. They're the 'what not to do' example for me."

One of Tom M.'s greatest concerns about aging is health—"health and mental health are major issues." Tom M. notes that he believes his "father didn't develop a severe drinking problem until he was in his 70s." Tom M. worries that aging has the "potential to put me down the same path as my Dad's. Maybe it's written in stone for me. Maybe its entirely genetic, who knows." Additionally, his mother has developed several health problems such as heart disease and diabetes. These are also problems Tom M. is afraid he will find out he has inherited.

Tom M. does think there are positive aspects of growing older. Among these positive aspects is "well-earned increasing freedom. . . . We have a lot of financial freedom now. And, another positive aspect to growing older is that, what with the kids grown up now, we have the freedom to travel and do things on our own schedule. This makes getting older a good thing. That's nice, it kinda' takes the edge off this aging thing."

Tom M. and his wife have been together since their early 20s; he has never been divorced or dealt with a significant breakup. Tom M. and his wife have made it clear to their children that "the expectation is that they take care of us. We've given them a very privileged life and provided them a foundation to create the same situation for themselves in adulthood. They need to reciprocate when we are older."

While Tom M.'s parents still live alone in their own home, he does contribute to their medical bills. Tom M. likes the concept of spending his entire adulthood "with one spouse, in one house, the way my parents have done." Tom M. emphasizes that he does not want to be alone when he gets older. "I've been with my wife for so long, I don't know what I'd do without her."

Story #25

Anton Y., Age 58

Anton Y. is a 58-year-old single male with two teen age children. He divorced five years ago, leaving his then wife of 15 years. He now lives alone, but has his children with him every other weekend, as per his custody agreement with his ex-wife. Anton Y. is a retired school principal.

Anton Y. says that getting "just a bit older than I was in my 40s" was hard at first, right after his divorce. "I was a bit lost. Didn't know what to do or who to be anymore. I noticed I slowed down in every way, physically, emotionally, mentally. Maybe it was the transition out of my marriage, which was hard back then." But in the recent couple of years, things have changed for Anton Y. "It's been great since I got over the divorce, because it's been like being a young bachelor again, but with the perks of being more mature." Anton Y. says that now he has the luxury of going on golfing trips with his friends, and enjoys all his free time. To Anton Y., "70 or 80 is old, but if I'm physically able, I'll still be golfing as often as possible."

Anton Y. doesn't expect his children to take care of him when he gets older, although he "would like to have the security to know they will if it is needed. After all, I don't have a wife anymore." Anton Y. feels that his children "are not going to be burdened by me, as I have enough of a retirement fund that it should cover anything I need. But of course I'd love to have the kids around." Anton Y. has never had to care for a parent or a grandparent he says, "so I have no idea what that's like.... Must not be very fun for anyone."

Anton Y. says that although he is dating, he has recently come to terms with the fact that he will most likely be alone as he ages. "Right after the divorce it worried me, but now I've learned to enjoy my time alone. And I will make sure the kids keep visiting me as much as they can." Anton Y. says he has a lot of friends in the "same boat as I am—divorced, older children, and lots of personal free time. Some of them don't know what to do with themselves. Others are thrilled. I'm in the thrilled group now, I think."

Anton Y. says that he and his friends can "age together, and it won't be as lonely." He notes, "So far, I haven't been worried about my friends not being able to stick around. Maybe someday this will be an issue, but not now. We're like a club."

Ben D., Age 66

Ben D. is a 66-year-old man who lost his wife five years ago, and does not plan to remarry. He says he knows one day he will be with his wife again, and for this reason he does not fear death. He lives "just day by day." Ben D. talks about aging as something he cannot quite understand: "I look in the mirror and am always surprised to see an older man, because I feel like I am 45, not 66. This face and this body are getting older, but I do not think I am. I've just stopped in time."

Ben D. describes his present life as "very contained, very predictable, very narrow, as these days I avoid anything much changing from day to day. I don't want any more upsets." Ben D. is visited by his adult children from time to time, and on holidays. He does not expect to be visited more than this. Ben D. says he is now "used to being alone a lot. And anyway, I might have to clean up the house or something, and I really don't want to have to change the way I live for company, or for family." Ben D. lives a very structured life. He "eats pretty much the same thing at the same time every day." He wakes up and goes to sleep "in the same bed at the same time every day."

Ben D. just retired six months ago. He says he is not very concerned about getting older, but that being alone in his home "sometimes feels a bit like being trapped. And it makes me uneasy, a kind of claustrophobia hits me." When he feels trapped, Ben D. says, he goes for a walk. "But sometimes," Ben D. adds, "sometimes I feel down, a sort of down mood creeping in on me. It's a strange down mood, kind of gritty, I can't describe it. I worry this is some sort of real bad depression I am getting into and that it will get worse as I am getting older. I'm not sure what to do about this or how to ward this off. I'll tell you one thing, sleeping pills aren't helping anymore. There are nights when I can't sleep and I can't stand being awake....But then there are times I am OK, so maybe it will get better. I always just wait 'til I feel OK again. I wait this rough time out."

Story #27

Jane Z., Age 60

Jane Z. is a 60-year-old woman, "still married, now for 20 years," to her second husband. Jane Z. and her second husband have three adult children, one together (born to them before they were married) and one each from each of their previous marriages. When asked whether she has given much thought to aging, Jane Z. replies, "Only this year, as our youngest is really out of the house (and we think none of the kids are moving back home), am I thinking about aging. Up 'til recently, I was too busy with working and family to think about my life at all. You don't really see getting older sneaking up on you. It's sort of like life happens and then here you are, 60. You turn around and wonder where time went, and then later you wonder where everyone went."

Jane Z. expresses a sort of empty nest "loneliness, with all the kids gone and so busy with their lives." She talks about her health and how she has not paid much attention to her minor health problems until now, and hopes they remain minor. Jane Z. says that she fears, "getting old and sick, and depending on people...and since you are using this interview anonymously, I will tell you that I do not think my husband would be there for me if I got very sick, as I am the one who takes care of everyone in this family. I have always been the caretaker, and everyone wants me to keep being the caretaker. Of course, so long as I am the caretaker, then it means that I am OK even if someone else is not, which I hope does not happen—I hope it does not happen that I will need to be taking care of people, and I hope it does not happen that people will need to be taking care of me, and I just hope everyone will be OK."

Jane Z. adds that her experience "living in the sandwich generation has been a demanding and painful time. Every one needed something from me for years, it seems for two decades. The second decade, it was parents needing me as much as kids did. And husband. I'm real tired." Jane Z. hopes that the money she and her husband have saved will last into and through their old age. "I hope our savings don't run out." She is concerned that her children, although now adults, will continue to need financial help from them (from Jane Z. and her husband), and "that this will drain the little we have saved away. Certainly, social security will not be enough, if it's there at all."

Jane Z. returns to the matter of her husband, who she says is "completely dependent on me for almost everything. I mean, he works, but is about to retire. I make more money than he does, and I pay for more of the bills than he does. And I take care of all the cooking and cleaning. What if I can't keep doing this forever, then what happens? And what if I tell him I will not do everything, take care of almost everything around the house and around the bills, for him forever, that I am too tired: will he leave me? I really don't know the answer to this."

Jane Z. pauses for a moment, and then she says, "I'm worried about something else, too....Well you see, I'm not as sharp as I used to be. I just don't know what it is. It is probably because I'm tired a lot so I don't think so clearly sometimes. I don't tell anyone, because what's there to say, because then this state of mind goes away and I can think again. Maybe I'm just over whelmed and have been for a long time....But these days, I can tell, I just don't think as quickly as I used to. I wonder what that is about."

Cristie S., Age 60

Cristie S. is a 60-year-old divorced woman, now single with a "boyfriend" as she calls him. Three of Cristie S.'s four children by her ex-husband are, she says, "grown and have families and careers of their own now. But the fourth, I worry about him. He's 32 and single and unemployed and still struggling with addiction to alcohol and drugs. He's been going through this for over 10 years. It's hard to keep watching and hard to keep helping."

Cristie S. has been divorced from the father of her children for 12 years, and says that she is "quite happy I made the decision to end that marriage when I did as it would be harder now, now that I am older. It seems that change is getting harder for me now, where before, when I was younger, I took changes easily. But I do feel that this divorce made it harder on that one son of mine who can't seem to find his way. But on the other hand, life got better for me after the divorce. I don't know how to see all this. Do I put myself first or my children before myself? I still wonder, even though they're adults and have been for a while."

Cristie S. has worked for a number of organizations and companies over the years, while also always maintaining part time self-employment. She feels confident that she can "keep making a decent living—but not forever." Cristie S. reports that "It is only now that I am starting to realize I am getting older. I've been so busy for so many years that I did not have time to notice even wrinkles on my face. Now suddenly, I see myself in the mirror and say but that is not me. I also am beginning to notice that I am starting to have problems with my knee and things like this. I guess this is aging, gee."

Cristie S. looks ahead and wonders what older age will be like for her. She is concerned about having what she needs to live on, to live well or "at least moderately comfortably" in her older years. Cristie S. notes that she has spent most of her retirement savings on her son's frequent addiction treatments. Cristie S. also comments that being alone or somewhat alone as she gets older is a "big concern" for her. She says she was always wanting more time to herself when there were so many work and family demands on her, but that now she is not sure she wants that time alone as much. "My desires have changed. I really do not want what I used to want in life. This is so strange, as I wanted what I wanted so badly, and now those things are not so important. My whole wish list has gotten shorter and been rewritten somehow.... I do wish I could spend time with my children and grandchildren, but not have to worry about any of them. I'm worried that I'm not going to be a lot of financial or emotional help to them as I get older. I'm exhausted."

Commentary

This fourth set of stories include interviewees whose ages range from 56 to 66. Now we see interviewees begin to reflect on their lives in an ever deeper way, with more looking backward on life added to the looking forward. (Clearly, enough life has now been lived to look back on.) What might they have done differently to prepare for their being this age or older? What did they not know about growing older when they were younger that they wish they had known then and do know now?

Notions of retirement, what it means, what it looks like, what it will cost, whether it will be possible, are coming on now, at least for some interviewees. Focus on what help to their parents adult children might be if help is ever needed is increasing. At the same time, there is still the concern regarding meeting or being able to meet children's—adult children's—needs. This concern lingers and even grows as children require a lot of not only love and attention but resources as well. How long will one's children stay fully or even partially dependent? What sort of attitude do these interviewees want to adopt regarding their children remaining dependent as they move into adulthood? What would be the best approach to take here? These are spoken and unspoken questions in the lives of these interviewees.

And, coping with the reality or possibility of divorce now or in the future, with the reality or possibility of being single now or in the future, with the reality or possibility of being alone now or in the future, are now more central concerns. Divorce represents many things to people at these ages. There is the failure-at-something perception, whether or not accurate, which can creep in. There are also the frequent (although not always present) great social, financial, and emotional costs of divorce, which take ever greater tolls on some persons as they grow older. Where many parents choose to stay together and forego divorce for the sake of their children, there is an unspoken question regarding what not getting a divorce when one is needed costs adults.

The creeping awareness that old age is not far around the corner is setting in. The rethinking of old goals, values and plans is being done. Ironically, when we finally pause to look back, we cannot go back and change the past. Well, can we change the present, some people ask. What is key at this time in these interviewees' lives is looking at the now, the present time, and even at the future while trying to maintain or finally find some sense of optimism. Optimism can make a great difference in the process of aging. However, the risk of depression is certainly present for a significant percent of all older people.

16

Mind-Brain Living through Aging

We are watching ourselves age. Perhaps we do not see ourselves standing on the sidelines of our major life aging process drama, however we know we are there, observing ourselves participating. Our brains recognize on some level the changes we and they are undergoing. Our brains feel the minor steps we take every moment of the aging process. After all, we and our brains are moving, second by second, millisecond by millisecond, through time.

Rarely do we ask ourselves how our brains will work when we are older, how we will think when we are older, and whether we will think as clearly as we do now then. These questions are dwelling deep inside us. However, with the exceptions of occasionally talking about "being forgetful" and of what we may joke are "senior moments," when we cannot find the phone number we wrote down earlier that day, we are not consciously examining our aging minds every step of the way.

The aging mind is a mystery, slowing revealing its answers to us. With life expectancies extending ever longer, there is time to see a growing number of persons walk the path of aging. The field of the psychology of aging is not yet as fully developed as is the well-developed field of child psychology, or as is the field of general across-the-generations adult psychology addressing mental health at any age (and special issues in young adulthood and midlife such as addiction, domestic violence, and divorce). However, increasing life expectancy is itself garnering increasing focus on the psychology of aging, and on the mind as it ages.

Already it is clear that general mental health can be maintained during aging as it can during any other part of life, and that psychotherapies, which are effective with young people and young adults, can be effective with middle aged and elderly persons as well. Even the rate of depression appears to be no larger for the elderly population than for people of younger adult ages. In fact, with the exception of Alzheimer's, the rates for most mental conditions and illnesses decrease with age. It is entirely wrong to assume that if one lives into her or his 80s, mental deterioration will be part of that process. Only a minority (although far too many) of those living into their 80s do experience such deterioration or Alzheimer's.

It is important to note here that older persons are at risk for a high rate of alcohol abuse and binge drinking, just as younger adults (and teens) are. More and more, we are finding that older persons may be quietly—without anyone knowing or caring—drinking alcohol, even drinking too much alcohol, many unaware of the impact upon them. In the face of growing awareness of and concern regarding the global alcohol overuse and addiction epidemic, we must not overlook alcohol problems among the elderly. Additionally, once people reach the age of 75, the impact of even average let alone excessive alcohol use is greater on the body and brain and has far more negative effects on mental functions such as cognition and memory. Older persons tend to be less aware of the impact upon themselves and others of any excessive alcohol use they may be engaging in. (For a more in depth discussion of excessive use and addiction, note that I have addressed alcohol and drug use patterns in great depth in my book, *Rewire Your Self to Break Addictions and Habits: Overcoming Problem Patterns*.)

Older persons are also heavy users of prescription drugs and over-the-counter drugs, largely but not always under doctor's orders. All too often, whether taken under one or more doctors' orders or simply self-administered in a self-medicating approach, drugs are combined or mixed in dangerous ways, unbeknownst to the elder persons using these drugs. (In some cases, this is the result of several different doctors prescribing medications without tracking what else is being prescribed for the patients elsewhere and what else is being taken over-the-counter by the patients.) The risks of both drug mixing and excessive alcohol use among the elderly are at least as if not more serious for older persons than for those of any other age.

Also note that while teens and younger adults with addiction problems have higher rates of buying or acquiring their drugs illegally, the elderly who are addicted tend to get most of what they use addictively quite legally. In fact, some (although not all of course) MDs are quite happy to

over prescribe pain killers, antidepressants, and other drugs, simply because they find it easier to over prescribe to older people than to face the
problems and challenges of treating them. It is as if society and the health
care industry looks away from the drug problems of older people simply because those problems do not rank high in the importance to them. Hence
the minds and brains and bodies of the elderly are at risk of addiction-like
problems, not simply because they are older but because they are so freely
and legally and even willingly drugged.

17

⤬

Social Isolation in Aging

Alone. No one to talk to, no ongoing relationships.

Some but not all older adults experience significant levels of isolation. Social isolation tends to increase with aging. One's social network may naturally grow smaller. One's social contacts may generally decrease in number and frequency, with fewer satisfying relationships being maintained. Additionally there is the increasing disappearance of friends, family, and long-term members of one's social network when these people move away or are moved away, grow infirm, or die of old age, accidents, and or for health related reasons.

Isolation is generally thought of as being a state of geographical (or at least locational) separation from others. Geographical can be replaced with social and perhaps even philosophical isolations with the same or similar outcomes—diminished number of social contacts or diminished number of meaningful social contacts. We can say quite logically that the fewer the meaningful social contacts (no matter what the reason), the greater the social isolation. Aging can be quite naturally accompanied by an increasing (although sometimes not entirely undesired) degree of social isolation stemming from one or more of these situations:

- lack of any or diminishing number of long-term friends
- lack of any or diminishing number of newer shorter-term friends
- lack of any or diminishing number of real contact events with short-term friends

- lack of any or diminishing number of primary relationship face time hours or real contact events
- lack of any or diminishing number of people in one's life
- lack of any or diminishing degree of emotional intimacy in any one relationship or in one's life overall
- lack of any or diminishing number of social contacts of any sort
- lack of any or diminishing participation in social activities
- lack of any or diminishing connection to locations and home or homes where many years of one's life were spent
- increasing dependence on someone (for driving, planning, making arrangements, and so on) just to be able to be in social contact with others

However, social isolation may in itself not be a problem. The issue may be more what is done with that social isolation than that social isolation itself. People who go into phases of social isolation with projects, agendas, fascinating pastimes, lines of work or other "occupations" are more prepared to not only weather but in many cases even benefit from a degree of stepping back or pulling in—which may or may not have the undesirable effects of unwanted social isolation. Note that Story 39 on page 174 in which Derrick G. explains how very much he likes his alone time, how very much he needs this time to paint his paintings, how very much he wants to be isolated when he is working, how very dependent upon his isolation he feels he is to paint, to do exactly what he wants to do.

For those less self-directed than Derrick G. (referred to above as per Story 39), social isolation in itself can have negative health effects. It is as if the mind—when not engaging in social interaction—is sending the body a message that it no longer needs to take care of itself, and quite possibly and sadly, that the self is no longer needed by the world. Where the brain is not being engaged in ongoing, regular social interaction of some sort, the brain may not be sending messages to itself to say stay engaged, stay involved, stay mentally alert and alive. The brain may not be reminding itself that what it has learned over many years of a long life is part of living, and is useful in the now. The brain may not be reminding itself that being engaged in interacting (or at least some degree of interacting) with others (at home, at work, at the store, and everywhere else) is central to living.

Quite possibly, it is not just the desire to feel needed that can be dimmed in the absence of an adequate degree of social interaction. It is also the desire of the body (and of the body's brain) to KNOW it is needed, to know it must engage socially with those it comes into contact with. The body and the brain want to have reason to send themselves messages that they are indeed needed. Here, the *will you still need me?* question is virtually biological, cellular, and biochemical. On a deep, cellular, even molecular level, we, our bodies and brains, are constantly registering the sensations of feeling less and less needed—at least in the ways we were needed at earlier times in our lives. The identity, at the least the old identity, is built on what the world seemed to need from us at earlier stages of life. With the world not needing the same things from us, and with us perhaps still needing the world to need the same things from us, we can experience what is a usually subtle yet profound identity crisis. Who are we now, who will we be tomorrow? (I see this questioning of the self in the aging process as it emerges within some of my clients. I suggest that they embrace this transition into the next phases of their lives. I suggest that they embrace this shift and find new areas for their identities to discover themselves as they are now, and as they are becoming. Ultimately we are talking about seeking a new relationship not only with the world, but with the self.)

18

Loneliness and Aging

Social isolation is not in itself loneliness, yet these are frequently confused. And loneliness itself is not necessarily part of aging; aging is not always accompanied by loneliness. Whatever one's age, loneliness can take it's toll on mental and physical health and well-being. Unhealthy effects of loneliness can be cumulative—the longer one is lonely, the greater the negative mental and physical health effects may be, especially in older persons. What can also be increasingly true as one ages is that the longer one is lonely, the more challenging it can be to reconnect with the world, to reduce or end the loneliness. We might see this as an adaptation to being lonely on an ongoing basis, an acceptance of loneliness perhaps, but it may also be more of a submission to the loneliness, which actually may also serve to perpetuate it. (It may also be the case that the way we deal with loneliness in our lives determines to some extent what the effect of this loneliness is on us.)

Before saying another word here, I again want to make clear: not everyone who is alone is actually lonely, or does get sick as a result of loneliness. Loneliness is a varying condition, with varying causes, and varying effects. Still, it is important to note that the effects of loneliness can be physical. This is not only an effect found in older age. Middle aged persons who have experienced divorce, especially women, and especially women who have lost custody of their children in a painful breakup, are actually at greater risk for heart disease than women in stable and happy family settings. (This does not mean that all stable family situations are happy. Refer again to chapters 14 and 15 for a discussion of how patterns, both positive and negative, can stabilize—become a way of life—over time.)

In older and even middle aged persons, loneliness is more prevalent among those who have lost a long-term spouse, as there is a pattern of living and relating that has been long established and then broken. There is also, almost literally, the risk of a broken or weakened heart (as health impacts of loneliness can include the heart). The detrimental effects of this loneliness can be greater among older persons, as they are less likely to re-engage with old social networks, or to establish new social networks, or to find a new mate for that matter.

Among older persons, there is a distinct correlation between degree of loneliness after losing a spouse and the length of the marriage or relationship one had with that spouse. Even where older persons live with their children after losing the long-term spouse, the degree of loneliness they experience can be quite high. Of note is the reality that when widowed persons live with siblings or other persons close to their own ages, they are somewhat less lonely after losing a long-term spouse. So while being able to move in with one's adult children may in many cases be wonderful and even necessary, there is also something to be said for living with one's elderly siblings (where there is already a history of lifelong connection and closeness—not all sibling relationships are like this).

One of the pathways of sensation where the emotional and physical effects of loneliness can overlap is in the stress response. Older persons who are lonely register more stress than do those who are not lonely. They actually test with higher levels of the well-known hormone and neurotransmitter, epinephrine, then those who are not lonely. This is not surprising, as a high degree of social isolation or loneliness (even loneliness we do not realize is affecting us) can be agitating on a deep instinctual level.

We are programmed to read signals regarding safety and danger, not only from our environments but also from the population or people around us. When we do not have full access to our environments and also do not have full access to the people we are used to reading for information about our environments, we are on a sort of subconscious yet tense alert. In these situations, the release of epinephrine is not surprising as it is used by the brain to rapidly boost the supply of oxygen and glucose—in order to quickly ready the body for any emergency response that could be needed.

Older persons who are lonely can be in a higher (and ongoing) state of agitated arousal. This state can have long-term negative health effects on the heart and other organs. Middle age and older persons who feel that they are lonely may tend to feel more helpless and threatened than do others, increasingly so as they age. Those who do not consciously feel they are lonely can nevertheless experience the psychological and physical effects of loneliness because this loneliness can register on a very deep level. Also of note, older persons are far less likely to seek help when feeling this way, whether they feel this subconsciously or consciously, or when feeling general stress itself. Experiencing loneliness, or anxiety and stress as a result of loneliness, older people are also more likely than others to see their present and past situations in a negative light. A combination of heightened stress and the lack of sleep that can accompany this stress can add to the wear and tear of aging on the body, mind, and soul. The internal biological and psychological anxiety over the question, *will you still need me?*, digs in deep.

19

---∞∞∞---

Living Environments, Health, and Well-Being in Aging

It is not surprising to find that the problematic combination of social isolation plus loneliness can have distinctly detrimental health effects, especially in old age. Some of the negative health effects of isolation and loneliness (ranging from physical disease states to chronic pain and other symptoms) appear to turn back or turn around or at least halt their progression, when some persons move into nursing homes. The level of social contact increases as a result of such a move, and indications are that health improvements appear with the increasing social contact these environments offer. In fact, following social isolation, even a minor increase in the level of social contact one is having in one's life can result in positive health changes. Messages are being sent to the mind and body that, wait, look again, I am still a part of the world; I am still in the world; I am needed to engage with the world, with people, at least this much if not more.

At the same time, being institutionalized does not sit well with all elderly persons, and many suffer from institutionalization syndromes such as depression, withdrawal, and loneliness itself. Also note that many "homes" elderly persons are moved into are virtually warehouses for the old. These environments do not produce positive health effects, lest there is any confusion regarding this. Some of these environments are downright unsafe both psychologically and physically. Every effort must be made to recognize the difference between a healthy elder living environment and one that is not. This of course includes looking at the quality of physical care and the physical safety of the environment, something too frequently neglected by some of the more warehouse type elder care environments.

But it also includes something that is also all too frequently neglected, the psychological well-being of the persons living in these environments. A healthy elder living environment includes a healthy psychosocial and interactional environment, which provides ample opportunities for appropriate social interaction, and where a person is treated with attention, interest and respect on an ongoing and regular basis. That these aspects should offer a psychologically sound elder living environment may sound obvious and may be expected of any elder living environment, Sadly these aspects are too often overlooked, either for reasons of ignorance or finance. (Consult the Sample Elder Living Environment Checklist in Appendix F.)

20

---◦◦◦---

Older Persons' Thoughts on Social Contact

Among older persons living alone who have been asked to interview for *Will You Still Need Me?*, many appear to want to talk, rather than to answer the specific interview questions listed in Appendix A of this book. The social contact and stimulation offered by these interview meetings is generally received with some degree of what appears to be positive excitement. Simply being visited appears to be quite a positive for these persons, and being told that their thoughts are wanted by the interviewer is clearly important to them. So these *Will You Still Need Me?* interviews in themselves offer not only social contact and interaction, but also a message that what these elder interviewees have to say is wanted, even needed. Here are some of the comments about life, views, items, experiences, family, and memories these interviewees volunteered:

- "I remember when my mother baked those cookies. We ate them when they were hot out of the oven."
- "I like to sit by the sea and just watch the waves. The sea makes me feel like I belong to the Earth."
- "I used to hate Bingo. But now, I like playing Bingo at the church, because I get to see the girls."
- "My family thinks I like holidays, but I don't. I wish they would just come over here, one by one, or just a few at a time, without everyone else. I like this better."

- "Since I don't hear very well anymore, I really don't like being where I cannot see someone's face. I feel left out when I can't hear."
- "I am a writer, and I am 80 years old. I am proud of myself. I like to keep my mind active. But I miss my family. They are working in other states."
- "It's good I have children and grandchildren, because I like knowing I am part of a family, my family."
- "I got lost when I walked to town the other day. I am afraid I am losing my mind.
- I am very afraid of being alone, even when people I know are with me, because maybe I won't know them."

V

‒‒‒⚬⚬⚬‒‒‒

THE MIND, LEARNING, AND MENTAL FUNCTIONING IN AGING

Too old to plant trees for my own gratification, I shall do it for my posterity.

—Thomas Jefferson

Mind Wants to Keep Working. Photo by and courtesy of Angela Browne-Miller.

Arle H., Age 65

Arle H. is a 65-year-old male, who, after three marriages and divorces, lives with his "significant other or partner of five years" as he describes her. Arle H. has "one biological son in his late teens from a previous marriage and one stepdaughter in her early 20s from this relationship." Arle says he is "generally OK with aging." Still, he says "there is something bothering me about getting older. This is seeing that each year now my old friends start to go one by one, and this can be a bit unnerving. This is a source of sadness and concern. It also leaves me a little lonely even though I have people in my life now. I try not to think about this too much though, so I don't dig into those feelings. I don't want to dig in as I might get stuck there with them, in that sad place."

Arle H. is a former military serviceman and state official. He now works full time in the private sector. About retirement, Arle H. says he will work for "three and a half more years. Even then, when I'm about 70, I really will not retire. It will be more like partial retirement, working at least part time on the job I have had for some years, and also working on the books and articles I want to write, the books and articles that I have not had time for yet.... I think not retiring is healthy. Although working yourself to the bone is not healthy either, so I do want to strike a balance."

When asked for his thoughts on Medicare and Social Security, Arle H. says, "These two programs are probably some of the best government programs ever put into action. I am so happy these exist."

Arle H. considers 80 "old" and says that "this is good, I will not be old for quite a while then." Arle H. does think about growing older although "being old" is a concern for him "to a point, but I think getting older is far better than the alternative, which is not being around to get older. I'll take getting older." Arle H. lists his "greatest concerns as per growing older" as "health, financial resources and financial stability, surviving family and friends, maintaining independence, and being alone.... Being alone would not be good for me. I am glad I have someone in my life." Arle H.'s previous divorces and relationship breakups have "made me realize that it is so easy to wind up being alone. You have to make an effort not to have that happen."

"Aging can be quite depressing if your health fails or if your money runs out," Arle H. says. He is "making every effort not to let that happen." Arle H. has watched other people age, and go through old age, and this has not been easy for him to see. Arle H. does hope that his children will not feel they have to take care of him when he is older, but does add that if he needs them, he knows they will be there for him.

Arle H. does think that there are positive aspects of getting older, which include "more time to accomplish goals and to travel, and also increased maturity, experience, wisdom, and patience. Patience is important. It took me a lot of my life to develop my patience to the point it is now." Arle H. does believe that having goals as he ages is a good idea. Arle H.'s goals for the coming years are to "write and publish at least half a dozen books, make a lot of money, travel, enjoy life and family."

Story #30

Arisha T., Age 65

Arisha T. is 65, lives with her two dogs, "no one else," and works full time. She does not feel financially secure enough to retire. Arisha T. says, "I am divorced. I would like to find a man to be in my life, but I don't think I will find one I can live with again. Most of the men I meet, if they really want to date someone their own age, then they want to settle down. But the thing is, they want someone to take care of them. Sounds like another job to me. I have had that job, taking care of a husband, before. It just doesn't pay."

Arisha T. feels that the trade off, being in a full time relationship versus having only herself to take care of, is easily figured out: she says she chooses being alone. "Not alone actually, as I have my two dogs, and they are really enough for me. Dogs are better than people because they always love you, always need you, never judge you, and never abandon you. . . . I need to be sure whoever is in my life will never abandon me. Otherwise, why bother? . . . Being left alone by someone is worse than being without someone in the first place. Anyway, I'm OK with my dogs. I can be with my own thoughts. The dogs don't really care how much time I like to spend just thinking about things these days, so long as they get their walk."

Story #31

Sten O., Age 68

Sten O. is a 68-year-old man. He lives alone and has lived alone since his divorce 15 years ago. Sten O. reports that as he grows older, he thinks "more and more about aging, something I gave no thought to until I turned 65. "Sten O. describes aging as a "scary process" but says that while he is scared, he does not worry about aging on a daily basis.

Sten O. also expresses these attitudes and concerns about aging: "People should think about aging a lot sooner in their lives than they do." "People should look ahead and try not to be alone when they are getting older, because it gets harder to find someone when you get older." "I have not retired yet, because I cannot afford to. So my job gives me contact with people, but I wonder what I will do when I can retire." "I wonder what it will be like to be getting older and older and being alone every single day."

Sten O. appears glad he is being interviewed. He says that he likes being interviewed as these questions, although they make him "a bit nervous about getting older," also make him think he should "do some planning, maybe join a club or a church or something. Or get married again. A wife is probably a good idea, now that I think about it. Or is it? Is a wife a good idea when you're getting old, can someone tell me?... Will a wife keep my mind and body from getting old, or just wear me out faster?"

Carla B., Age 67

Carla B. is a 67-year-old woman, married mother of five grown children, who has several grandchildren. Carla B. says she has "been gifted with a wonderful long-term marriage." Carla B. met her spouse in her late teens. They later married and "have been together ever since." Carla B. looks at aging as "something that is happening to everyone, so we are all doing it, and this makes it a bit easier. Since everyone looks older, it's like we don't see ourselves getting older alone." She feels that "it is good to have the same friends around for many many years. It's like family."

Carla B. expresses concerns about moving into her early 70s because "70s IS getting old and many health concerns start to show up there." She is concerned about her hip and her knee "giving out and making it hard for me to get around." Carla B. does not want people to have to take care of her, as she feels she has "always been the one to take care of everyone else." Carla B. has been the primary babysitter for all her grandchildren. Carla B. is also the main source of care and company for her parents and her husband's parents. "All this caring for people has been a lot of my life for a long time. I need to have someone else take over all this work for me, but who?"

Carla B. does worry about being lonely in older age. She has watched her mother-in-law "grow increasingly lonely" as her father-in-law grows older and says this loneliness is her mother-in-law's "major problem." Carla B. says that she does not want to "end up like that." Instead, she says, she wants to develop "a passion, something that I do and like to do, that does not directly involve my family, something that is all about me. I need this to keep going now and feel like these is a future." Carla B. adds that she naturally keeps her mind sharp by reading and by playing board and card games. She says she "actually love games. I think I'm addicted to them in a good way."

Story #33

Giselda A., Age 73

Giselda A. is a 73-year-old woman, a grandmother of three, who dresses very stylishly, wears all the most recent fashions, has a slim trim figure, dies her hair to cover "all the grey," and is frequently mistaken for "50 something," which she says she greatly enjoys. Giselda A.'s husband is just a few years older, however he appears much older and is frequently mistaken for being 10 to 15 years her senior (when she appears to be 50 something), a mistake Giselda A. also greatly enjoys.

Giselda A. says she was considered a great beauty in her "home country" when she was a teen and young adult, and she is proud of this. "I could not be happy if I lost all my looks!" she exclaims. "How I look is a lot of who I am, who I have been all my life. Getting old does not mean I cannot still be beautiful, does it? It's mostly how you feel about yourself."

Giselda A. does worry about being alone in later life. She says she hopes that she and her husband "go at the same time, so I will not be here without him, the way so many other women are without their husbands. Being an old woman without a husband is not something I want to be." Giselda A. does not know whether her family would be able to take care of her if her husband could not, as "he has always taken care of me, he has handled all that, and I do not know what to do about business things. I don't even know how to live a day without him. I'm just not as smart as he is, you know. He is good at everything and I, well I am just beautiful—as long as I can be."

Story #34

Rene M., Age 78

Rene M. is a 78-year-old woman who lives with her 53-year-old daughter, Leslie, her 60-year-old son-in-law, Donald, and the one of their children (Kenny, who is now 28) who still lives at home and worries his parents in this regard. Rene M. has other grown children, however, this daughter, Leslie, is the only one of her children who asked Rene M. to move in with her when Rene M. turned 73 and had broken her hip. Once Rene M. moved in with Leslie while recovering, she never again has left her daughter's home.

Rene M. says she is not sure why she "stayed with Leslie like there was nothing else I could go do," as she was "totally fine once recovered," however her daughter "absolutely insisted and that was that." Rene M. shares what little income she draws from Social Security with the "family pot." She lives in the home, in the "in-law apartment" that Leslie gave up (it had been Leslie's office) for her mother to live in. Rene M. worries that someone or ones in the household are, as she says, "not entirely happy with the situation, but no one says anything to complain and everyone is very nice to me."

Rene M. describes "getting older" as a "strange process, because you don't know how the next year or day will be. The future is always a mystery. You start to wonder if you'll stay the same or change...what if I break another bone, or...? What if I can't keep thinking real well? How much patience will my family have with me then?"

Walt M., Age 68

Walt M. is a 68-year-old man who has been married "for many decades" and has five adult children and six grandchildren. Walt M. recently retired, after working as a professional throughout his adulthood, since his mid 20s. Walt M. is proud of the fact that he worked hard and saved well, and has been able to "retire comfortably and finally start to really enjoy life."

Walt M. had planned everything quite carefully, and was certain he could retire comfortably, or he would not have retired. However, since he retired, for the first time since his now grown children left home, several of his children need financial help from him. Two have lost their jobs. One is underemployed after a cutback at work. Walt M. is now providing financial assistance to all of his five children, two of whom have their own children, which makes their financial need all the more pressing for Walt M. "I can't let my grandchildren go without, nor my children, can I?"

Walt M. is certain that he must help. "I never spoiled my children growing up and certainly not once they completed college. I made no room for anything but for their going out and finding good jobs and getting their own places to live. And all of them have done very well at this, they have never until now asked me for anything much.... But times are different now, and I just do not know who would help them if I did not. I didn't resent it, but it does weigh heavily on me. It's a lot of pressure."

Walt M. is most concerned that his hard earned nest egg is going to shrink to a "dangerously low point," and that he will not be able to be "comfortably retired" as he had planned to be all these years. Walt M. is even considering going back to work, however he says, "If I do unretire myself, I will have a hard time getting my clients back, and a hard time getting new clients. And I am too old to start all over again. I really do not know what to do. I'm not sure I can generate new income now. If I can, it won't be anywhere near as much. And my mind is just not quite as good as it used to be. It still works, however I don't think as quickly or clearly as I used to. Maybe I'm just tired or overwhelmed by everything and my mind is fine,... I just don't know for sure. What happens to everyone if I can't help them all anymore?"

Commentary

This set of stories includes interviewees whose ages range from 65 to 78. Now a sense of what one's future may or could be like is somewhat clearer, at least for some people. Yet, new questions about the future may be only now emerging. For some, financial, marital, and or health statuses feel to be more known, more clear, now, whether or not these actually are more clear. Is the now front and center reality of growing older clarifying things or is it simply becoming so very front and center that questions about what aging will be someday are not asked as frequently? Acceptance of unknowns may be more common. For many people in this age range, the reality emerges that they cannot know for sure what their financial, marital, and or health statuses will be in the future. It is not accurate to assume that these things are always more certain with age, especially when an economy can wobble in unexpected ways.

For many in this age range, being alone or facing the possibility of being alone takes on still more meaning. What does it mean to be alone financially? What does it mean to be alone in other ways—on holidays, in daily life, in making decisions.

The possibility of losing certain capabilities is also emerging. Whether or not this concern is based on reality is secondary to the concern itself. Now, ways to keep the mind and body active and working are all the more important. What can we do to stay alert, healthy, and alive? We realize how much we value our minds as we age.

21

⊷

The Brain Does Age

There is no way (yet) of getting entirely around this aging thing, even in the realm of the brain. The brain, just as the rest of the body, does age. Science is telling us that aging does affect attention and memory as well as spatial and sensory (such as vision and hearing) abilities. However, take heart. We are learning more about the resilience (ability to come back from deterioration and or damage) of the brain, at least under some circumstances. Where science will take us we cannot know, however we can likely look forward to breakthroughs in the preservation and stimulation of the brain well into old age.

Let's consider the brain, and its marvelous scope of work. The human brain is a symphony of bioelectrochemistries, flowing through the brain's magnificently mysterious synapses (despite all science knows about these). The synapse is the connection between neurons (cells that are key components of the brain, the spinal cord, and the nervous system). Synapses are found between neurons and between neurons and brain cells. The human brain contains from 100 to 500 trillion synapses, located among some 100 billion neurons. These synapses are essential to just about everything the brain does, such as the biological workings of our perceiving, experiencing, reacting, reasoning, and other sending-thinking and related acting. (Synapses are the junctions through which neurons signal each other and other cells by means of electrochemical signaling. In the brain, the "synapse," the gap between brain cells, is the site of perhaps greatest importance, the site through which the electrical impulse within a cell can trigger the release of a neurotransmitter, which can trigger electrical activity across the synapse and in the next cell.)

The brain's ability to make all this work, and to think based on all this, is a feat of sheer bio-organizational prowess. Among the countless marvels the human brain functions perform are:

- attentional functioning (the ability to pay attention to something, and to choose what to pay attention to)
- learning processes (both simple and more complex procedures the brain undertakes to learn something, to remember what is learned, and also to use it later)
- problem-solving procedures (both very simple and more complex)
- decision making—that all-essential functioning involved in choosing to get up in the morning let alone to do anything else in life

All of these functions and more are directed by a powerful, omnipresent sort of *executive control function* that the brain establishes to run itself. With practice, the brain hones, better directs, the bioelectrochemical processes it performs. The brain and the mind it houses learn bits of information that are then tied together into longer networks of learned and processed and stored information. Steps for working with and acting upon this information are learned—in children this learning is done largely but not always by experiencing (this does work, this does not work) and by mimicking (being taught by parents and teachers and friends who both model and directly teach these steps). In older people, these steps for working with and acting upon information must continue to be initiated, stimulated, and followed through on. We do not want to lose the capacity to take these mental dot-connecting steps. How do we preserve this capacity as we age, when as we age we mimic less, and maybe also experience less (in the outer world)? So what is an aging person to do?

First, it helps to know what our brains are, or should be, busy doing while we are too busy to notice. It helps to notice, to pull these processes into our consciousness as much as we can, to keep them consciously in use. The brain employs various means of initiating steps for acting on learned information such as these processes:

- logical thinking processes such as deduction (taking a big picture or idea or concept and from this, figuring out about the smaller parts that form it)

- logical thinking processes such as induction (taking small parts of a whole picture or idea or concept and from those, seeing the whole picture or idea)
- other logical thinking processes such as association

Much of the learning we do is accomplished by connecting dots, seeing relationships between the countless bits of information we have stored. This is learning by association or *associative learning*. Transferring what is known about one thing to what is then known about another thing takes place ever more frequently and at ever higher conceptual levels as the child's brain matures and then as the adult's brain accumulates more and more transfer experiences. There is no reason for these and other mental processes to slow or stop as we age. We can and must continue to ask our minds to connect dots, and to look for a-ha's.

These are magnificent processes. We must honor our brains for what they can and do achieve. But we may wonder: can the complex processes of learning and thinking go on forever? Do these processes wear down as we age? Does the brain age? Does it stop learning? Do the brain's (mind's) abilities to oversee its own processes by means of executive control functions diminish over time? Do the brain's wonderful abilities—to focus attention, to learn simple and complex things, to problem solve, to make decisions, to associate, to transfer knowledge—weaken or fade away or deteriorate or flat out stop working as we age? Can we keep our mind-brain's executive control function alive and highly functional? Yes, why not? We have to make a conscious decision to do so.

The above can be troubling questions. Certainly some degree of cognitive impairment may accompany aging. However, it is also true that some of the greatest thinking ever done by human beings has been done by those over 50, over 60, over 70, and maybe even over 80 and 90. Where once we believed that 50 was generally quite old, we now frequently describe judges and professors and scientists as being "at the top of their game" at the time of life from 50 to 70 or even 80. And ever more frequently, we are seeing judges and politicians, poets and artists, professors and researchers, stretch their productive years well into their 70s and continue to publish and contribute into their 80s (and sometime even beyond). Retirement age itself is raising near age 70, and maybe will even surpass 70, and not merely for financial reasons; clearly many persons are quite able to work and to contribute well past previously recognized as acceptable and expected retirement ages.

And note that the responses to these questions (about the brain and aging) that modern neuroscience is offering are not necessarily troubling.

Sure, it seems to be true mature adults lose tens of thousands of nerve cells a day, maybe 50,000 a day. It has appeared to be true that the brain does not regenerate these, although neuroscience is now seeing that neural growth—the generation of new nerve cells—can and does take place in adults, at least in selected areas of the brain. Nerve cells, serving as the core components of the brain, regenerate when nearby neurons are damaged. Neurons appear to pick up the slack when neighboring neurons stop functioning or stop functioning well. Neurons appear to grow new synaptic connections where old ones fail. These are good signs! It turns out that our brains are quite resilient, quite neuroplastic.

What is most important here is that neurons apparently can and do continue to grow and adapt their work (develop new neuronal-synaptic connections) well into adulthood. What is also important here is that new pathways can be and are grown when new experiences and new learnings are encountered. In fact, mental abilities can be stimulated at most any time in life. Science may one day have a pill to give us to keep our brains healthy well into old age, and perhaps even treatments for bringing receding mental abilities back to life. In the mean time, and even once there is this sort of pill, exercising the mind is at least as important as exercising the body throughout life. Challenges, riddles, games (and even video games), problem-solving procedures, and more can and should continue into later life.

So you need your brain to stay active! Never stop learning, never stop thinking, never stop pushing the brain to use itself. This does not mean that everyone over 60 should return to school to learn advanced physics. This does mean that there are many ways of stimulating one's brain to work, to challenge itself, in later life. Where someone might find physics the solution, another might find chess the solution. Some older persons, even in their 80s, are indeed going back—successfully—to school, studying computers and art and even law. (There are even law students in their 80s these days.) Learning new things in middle age and in older age has a stimulating effect on the brain and on the self. Ongoing learning says to the brain: *Hey, we still need you!*

The human brain holds infinite mysteries. Among the mysteries are those of the aging person's brain. What as yet unrecognized and even undiscovered wisdoms, talents, and capabilities may be housed in a generation or several generations full of brains whose full potentials remain as yet untapped? Dare we miss out on this much mental potential? Does the ever growing population of people over 60 carry an untapped massive mental potential and wisdom? (I believe so, and say that just like other magnificent resources, these have to be discovered, protected, and nourished!)

22

———∞∞∞———

Inner Thinkings and Age

It may be a surprise to hear that mental development can continue as we age. In fact, this ongoing mental development is virtually essential. We want to continue to stimulate our minds, to ask these minds to explore new subjects, to see new relationships between ideas, to solve new problems, to think in new ways, to connect old knowledge to new knowledge, and to see new connections among points of old knowledge that may otherwise never be used again.

The withdrawal from the world we think of as typical of old age is not necessarily typical and not necessarily necessary unless desired. Where the older person appears to onlookers to withdraw, this may be an illusion. Or, it can be that this person is indeed less and less engaged; that mind may be less and less involved in the outer world—the surrounding world. Of course disengagement is our right, the right of those disengaging as they age when they choose to, and when they are truly involved in the choice to disengage. However, a great deal of the disengagement we see is actually a pulling back because no one told us staying engaged was an option—or that staying engaged while aging was very important to be doing. Much of the time, we actually do have a choice regarding whether we recede from the world, and if we do, the rate of receding and the degree to which we recede from meaningful interactions. These meaningful interactions can of course be with others—social (as discussed in chapters 17 and 18), and they can also be with the self, with the mind, as discussed in this chapter (as well as in chapters 24 and 25). Interaction with the mind is of course both interaction with the self and interaction with the world as it involves thinking, interacting with ideas, with issues. In fact, many people never recede from meaningful interactions with thinking, ideas, issues—the world.

We cannot control everything that takes place in our lives. Similarly, we cannot control everything our minds and brains do. Yet we can have a significant say in how much we do to keep our minds working, and working well. We must ask our selves—*will we still need our minds as we age*—will we still call upon our minds to think for us and to think a great deal for us? And we must answer—yes, we will still call upon and need and want our minds to work for us as we grow older.

Much research has gone into the development of mental abilities in children and teens. (I in fact have contributed to this thinking and research in my book, *Raising Thinking Children and Teens*, where I discuss how very important it is to stimulate young people's minds, and to teach them to think, and to learn. Ideally, we can take this advice, and apply this to adult persons as they age, as many of these strategies for stimulating the mind hold no matter what age we are.)

For example, we can continue to ask ourselves (our minds) to develop and apply mental strategies for working with information. We can continue to develop and apply organizational skills in our lives and in our thinking. We can continue to develop verbal abilities, and mathematical abilities, and musical and spatial awarenesses. We can continue to exercise our concentration and focus abilities. We can work against the withdrawal of brain speed and memory functions by asking our minds to continue to use and exercise these functions.

This may all sound rather lofty and perhaps even too demanding for aging minds. However, aging minds can want stimulation, can crave stimulation, and can ride the aging process better with stimulation. Aging minds, as all other minds of persons of all other ages, want to think, and want to have the opportunity to "figure things out."

We have to focus on the existence within each of us of a level of thinking—a sort of master level—above just thinking directly about the subject or issue at hand. This is the level we want to remember to keep alive and working. We still, we always, need this master level, the brain's executive control function, no matter what our age may be. This master or executive level manages many functions and processes at the same time. Many of these we engage in automatically, such as the beating of the heart, or the solving of an urgent time pressing problem, when only an immediate response will be useful. Others of these we engage in when we tell ourselves to, such as adding up the charges on a grocery store receipt. We carry within our minds a control mechanism that organizes all these processes, and even selects what processes to apply when. This control mechanism, a sort of mental director or executive control function, chooses what problem-solving processes and what other thought processes to apply when. Choosing the addition function to add up charges on a grocery store receipt is done by this mental control mechanism.

Clearly, when the mind is not used, its functions can rest unused and perhaps atrophy, deteriorate, or fade. (Use it or lose it.) Similarly, it is quite likely that the mind's control function itself must continue to be utilized—consciously and purposefully utilized. Even applying a mental strategy is a thought process, a mental discipline. The PROCESS of thinking something through and talking about it as you do is as important as the OUTCOME of this process. It's all about the mind and brain working, fully alive.

23

Problem-Solving Strategies
and Aging

One of the ways we can stimulate our mind's executive control functions as we age is to play challenging games, crossword puzzles, card games, and other games that require the mind to select and apply strategies. We want to remind ourselves, even to teach ourselves, to think about the *concept* of a problem-solving strategy. Just talking about strategy, such as about strategy in playing a complex game, paves the way for a greater understanding and continued use of it. When we think about strategies for problem solving, for thinking things through—whether these things be real life situations or mock ups such as those posed in games—we exercise the mind. We exercise the control mechanisms of the mind by having the mind actively have to select problem-solving strategies and adapt these to ever different, even if only somewhat different, situations.

Applying problem-solving strategies cannot be underrated in keeping our minds working for us. In this effort, the executive control function of the mind is working, is exercising, is sending and receiving messages from various parts of itself. This is great exercise for the executive control function, and it is also a way of stimulating otherwise unused and otherwise never used (in some cases where what is being done is quite new) pathways in the brain. We now know that encouraging young people to problem solve is good for them, that this contributes to their mental and even emotional development. Who would have thought that the aging mind benefits from this same type of stimulation? Well, of course, we all know this.

Thinking Through Problem-Solving Steps

Step: Consider the Reason for Being Presented with this Problem

Step: Assess the Level of Difficulty of this Problem

Step: Note Your Degree of Familiarity with this Problem

Step: Judge the Type of Problem

Step: See this Problem in Your Mind

Step: Try it on for Size (Physical Imaging)

Step: Connect this Problem to Personal Experience in the Material
World

Step: Build on Experience

Step: Apply Relevant Principles

Step: Break the Problem into Small Steps

Step: Build on Others' Findings

Step: Build on Your Own Findings after Doing All the Above

Step: Use Everything Available to You to Think this Through

Even reviewing, relearning, or learning for the first time, to problem solve in different and even new situations can stimulate the mind at most stages of life. And yes, we want to continue to problem solve, but we also want to continue to consciously and purposefully see ourselves problem solving. Consider learning problem-solving steps such as these listed in the table at the end of this chapter, whatever your age, even putting a chart listing these steps on the wall at home, if memorizing and then using these steps is not easy for you. Simply consciously trying to apply this step-by-step problem-solving process to practical and even personal situations is good mental exercise. Adding to this exercise the effort to apply this step-by-step problem-solving process to more than one large or small challenge a day is even better mental exercise. Add to this effort a process of reviewing one's problem-solving behavior and learning from this review, adds still more to learning. This is because having the mind *think about its thinking process* at any age, even older age, is highly valuable. (Note: further discussion of the problem-solving steps in the following table is included in Appendix B.)

24

Rethinking through Things and Mental Aging

Give your self words to think about, words that will stimulate your thinking. Consider concept-related words such as "strategy," "complex," "abstract," "fragile," "absurd," chaotic," and any other conceptual words that come to your mind. Unpack these words in your mind. Think of their meaning. Keep a notebook to help you remember what words and concepts you are thinking about. Don't make this a high pressure "I must learn this now" activity. Keep this fun—no pressure. Don't worry if you didn't start thinking about words early in your life, it is never too late to begin. Add more challenging words to your list, maybe one a day. Expand your vocabulary potential simply by using certain words again and again. And then, consciously review, think, about how you use and reuse these words.

And keep your mind young enough to explore and to rethink—reformulate—what it already knows. Reformulation is a revision of your present way of thinking about or through something, or a new understanding of a particular word, definition, function, or process. New ways of seeing the same old things keep these new. They also keep the mind young. We need to continue to see new aspects of the same things, ideas, and relationships. We also need to continue to see new things, ideas, and relationships. The mind must be encouraged to keep looking at the world in new ways, despite the counterpart need for regularity and predictability in our environments as we age. (Both needs can be satisfied concurrently.)

And work to keep your spatial awareness alert and alive. Spatial ability develops and continues to develop with our experience in space, in the space around us we call our environment. Spatial ability is the ability to relate areas, objects and their shapes and sizes to each other. Although much of the learning in this area is learning by doing, there is also a lot to be said for learning by thinking. We are never too old to ask ourselves, "Do you think that will fit there?" This question triggers wondering, contemplation. Our mind *sees* the problem in reality (the yarn that will or will not fit through the eye of the needle, the puzzle piece that will or will not fit next to another piece, the desk that will or will not fit under the window, etc.). Our mind also sees, visualizes, *builds a mental construction* of, the problem or situation. We have been visualizing all our lives. Let's not stop thinking like this as we age.

And keep thinking about numbers as well. Life is full of opportunities to think in numbers, opportunities for mathematical analysis. Take advantage of opportunities to do number thinking. Regardless of your age, you can regularly be counting, measuring, adding, estimating, and undertaking other number-related procedures. Double check restaurant bills, calculate miles per gallon of gas your car is getting, balance your checkbook, calculate the down payment on your house, and so on.

And music, yes keep music in your life. Music is a key to the heart, the soul, the mind, and even the body. Music is tone and rhythm. A rhythm is a repeated sound pattern, a repeating beat. Continue to hear and or feel rhythm, see how it helps the mind continue to relate to and recognize patterns. Pattern recognition is an essential mental activity, valuable in reading, mathematical reasoning, and abstract thinking—valuable in living.

Verbal skills can be stimulated by learning songs at any age. Play the same songs again and again for yourself. Begin learning, remembering new songs as you age, and keep learning the words to these new songs. Words are more readily remembered when they are remembered to music. This stimulates memory as well as other mental functions at the same time. In memorizing even bits and pieces of songs, the mind opens storage compartments, stimulates new and old areas of itself.

25

---∞∞∞---

Learning to Learn Again,
in Later Years

Keep thinking. Always. Keep thinking as you age. And keep the mind organizing ideas and information. Even organize things, objects, for mental exercise. Organizing objects by size, color, purpose, age, value, or other categorical divisions requires that the mind organize ideas and concepts. Take advantage of both real and invented needs for mental and actual organization. Sort knives, forks, and spoons into separate containers. Organize colored chips and cards by color and type. Do this for fun, and for your mind-brain.

Keep your mind alert enough, perceptive enough, to notice large and small changes and differences in the world around you. Identifying large and small differences among things (and ideas) is part of thinking and of continuing to *learn to think*. The organization activities referred to in the above paragraph involve *differentiation*. Unless one can tell the difference between things being sorted, they will all fall into the same category. Look for opportunities to distinguish between types of dogs, flowers, books, foods, and so on. Look also for opportunities to observe finer differences such as those among flowers on the same bush or among petals on the same flower.

Even be sensitive to differences among differences: "That shoe and this shoe are a bit different from each other, but that shoe and that very tiny shoe are even more different from each other." When you are on the freeway (and someone else is driving), notice how cars are moving at different speeds. Look for cars that are moving at very different speeds from each other and also at very different speeds away from each other. See the *differences between differences* as much as possible: see *relative differences*. This keeps active a slot in the mind for advanced comparison and abstract thinking.

Continue to find reasons to concentrate as you age. Sometimes we forget the importance of our focusing, concentrating, although we do recognize this importance for children, as if children's learning is important while older learning is not. This assumption could not be more incorrect. (Note: our children may specialize—develop expertise—in something very early and stay with it for many years—as we see young Olympic gymnasts do. Or, children may delve into something for a while and then move on. Parents too often chastise children for "not staying with anything long enough" and should be careful about this criticism. If parents feel themselves applying intense pressure and or anger or bribery to get their children to stick to things, a step back should be taken right away. What is the real goal of all this? This is not to say that giving up on an activity, or on several activities in a row, is to be favored. However exploration and experience is valuable, quite often at least as valuable as the outcome of—violin, piano, drum, and so on—lessons themselves. It turns out that exploration and learning, trying to learn new things as well as further learning old, is also valuable as we age, at all stages of life, older ages as well. The end result is secondary to the process of exploration, so explore.

Experiences learning to concentrate can be built over time, and it is never too late to begin. Start now, or start again now, whatever your age. Each experience learning to concentrate—and continuing to learn to concentrate—on something in particular allows us to learn and keep learning:

1. to engage in repeated, sustained, and cumulative goal-oriented concentration over a period of time
2. to have confidence in our ability to focus
3. to apply variable concentration skills that can be transferred to other activities

Concentration skills are valuable at all ages. While childhood is a great time to begin learning to concentrate deeply, it is truly never too late to begin, to start concentrating on concentration itself. In fact, older people tend to realize how special concentration is, while children may or may not. You CAN teach even an old dog some exciting new tricks. Thinking skills CAN and should be continuously taught, learned, and practiced.

One of the essential elements of concentration education is the understanding of the essence of concentration. Ask yourself what you think the definition of concentration is. Then check your mind out—do it NOW—how closely are you concentrating on what you are reading here? How do you know? What can you do to *focus in* on this activity—this reading—right now? Are you focusing? (By the way reader, what did you think of just now when you read the word "focusing"—and what are you thinking of now that I ask this?)

Survey your knowledge of your own concentration activity as follows:

- Have you ever been aware that you were concentrating intensely on something?
- Exactly how did you come to realize this?
- On what were you concentrating so intensely?
- What types of activities do you concentrate intensely on?
- Do you allow yourself to be distracted when you really do not want to concentrate?
- Are there particular times of day and places in which you concentrate best?

You can continue to improve the workings of your mind by always practicing concentration. Your attention span can even lengthen. You ability to work with complex ideas can even increase. Your mental confidence can even expand.

Memory skills are also invaluable. Memory plays a critical role in learning, and in ongoing learning. Without memory, what can be learned can be lost. There are many scientific explanations for memory and learning. We can generalize or simplify them here this way: Bits of information are taken into the mind and held in the short-term memory. This information is examined, applied, its use repeated, until it is permanent enough to be moved into the permanent or long-term memory.

Memory can be strengthened with practice. Try to build these memory practice methods into your life. Don't pressure yourself, just practice these things:

- Memorizing sayings and poems
- Remembering a series of events in detail

- Remembering where things have last been seen
- Remembering a whole story or a speech

Think for a moment about your mind's speed. Brain speed is the speed at which electrical impulses or signals move across the brain from one point to another. Again, a brain can be and should be exercised at all ages, even into older age—even its brain speed should be stretched and made to work. Just as you can strengthen your memory, you can cultivate your brain speed. Runners who sprint in short running competitions practice to increase speed. Thinkers—anyone using their brains—can practice to increase brain speed. Try activities such as these:

- Play games that encourage quick responses. Find a game or an object that has a light that blinks suddenly. Even a flashlight with a blinker button will do. (Have someone flash the light repeatedly, or get a blinking light if no one is available to assist.) Require yourself to do something immediately upon seeing the light go on. If you are playing a manufactured game, such a requirement may be built in. Otherwise, create opportunities for yourself to practice responding as rapidly as possible to a stimulus such as a light that suddenly and unpredictably blinks. The required response should be an easy one, involving a small motion of the hand or a tap of the finger. Do this type of practice regularly. Adults of all ages benefit from such practice, so do not avoid it.
- Play games that encourage quick thinking. You can even play "easy" games for this purpose. The goal here is getting KNOWN answers rapidly, retrieving known information, not measuring whether or not you can get them right.
- Play games that encourage quick responses and quick thinking, and also new thinking and learning. Challenge the mind's reaction time and response time, and also its ability to connect dots—connect bits of information together to arrive at new information. (Many new challenging video games are good sources of such multiply challenging activities.)

Continue this way whenever you find a chance. I am actually talking about a state of mind here: Once you begin looking for opportunities to stimulate your mental abilities, you will find these everywhere. Have fun with this process.

And then there is creativity. Intelligence finds its way into expression via creativity. We often overlook the role of creativity in the expression of mental activity. Instead, we see only the most obvious signs of creativity, the most innovative inventions, the newest science fiction films, and so on. We notice children's wildest stories, brightest paintings, and loudest projections of their creativities. Yet creativity is manifested in most every expression of the mind. Just turning an idea into an expression of that idea requires creative energy. Thinking about taking a drink of juice and then lifting the glass to one's lips and sipping the juice requires an ingenious *transformation of thought into action*.

However, this and most simple actions like it are so common and so automatic that we rarely appreciate this transformation. Still, the things we do, the efforts we make, the thoughts we think, are the body of creativity. Life is a creative process. Even the most simple, common acts are creative; all transformation of ideas into efforts or actions is creative. This means that you are always and already *a creative being*. You are merely providing yourself activities that express and enhance your creativity. Keep doing so.

Keep seeing relationships between ideas and pieces of information. Once information has been stored in memory by the brain, it must be retrieved to be used. Retrieval usually involves some form of connection or association between whatever task the individual is performing and the stored (previously memorized) information. For example, if I ask a first or second grade child to tell me what 86 plus 1 is, that child may be reminded of other (blank) plus one type of questions. Knowing that one more than 10 is 11 and one more than 12 is 13 is helpful. Knowing that 6 plus 1 is 7 is still more helpful. The memory, 6 plus 1 is 7, is triggered by the sound of 80-*six plus one*. The memory of adding one to any number is triggered by the sound of *plus one*. The mind connects the task at hand to previously stored information.

When a more complex task is presented, such as, "think of a living thing that has fins but is not a fish," the mind must recall quite a bit of information. (1) A living thing is an animal or a plant. (2) A fin is a flat, arm-like part of some animal's body. (3) Plants do not have fins. (4) Fish have fins. (5) Seals and whales also have fins. (6) A seal is not a fish. (7) A whale is not a fish. Now the mind is retrieving several bits of information, each of which it may have learned and stored in memory at different times, under different circumstances, for different reasons. A young person might have learned the term "living things" in school. She or he might have learned about fins on a family trip to the zoo. Other information may have come in at other times. The child must relate the question being asked to information taken in at other times and then put it all together. So must the adult. The more that a piece of information is connected, interconnected, to other information, the greater the chance it will be retrieved, remembered. We can help ourselves become conscious of the importance of connecting information by looking at how bits of information can be connected to each other. Just talking about connecting thoughts helps us become more aware of the possibilities of doing so. Make this a recurring conversation with yourself and others over time, over the years, as you age.

The ability to connect or *associate* information is applied so frequently, and is so ever-present that we rarely think about it. However, we can encourage this ability in ourselves, even keep it alive in ourselves. We can encourage the skills that this ability depends on in ourselves. The connection of what may be otherwise unconnected ideas, concepts, or images is a creative act. This requires *the creation* of a link between bits of information. Learn to create these links, and keep the mind adept at creating these links. No matter what your age:

- Look for links that can be made.
- Play association games such as I'm thinking of something big and red that starts with an "a" (for apple).
- Play sentence and story completion games.
- Play charades and other games in which there is the challenge to decipher and express messages.

Again, never stop learning. Learning is a creative process. It is also a selective process: The mind, in its natural creativity, *selects* information to be operated upon and stored. We can call this process of selection and storage "learning." Adults' minds can continue to be attentive to this remarkable process of selection and storage, of learning. We can and must *learn to learn* throughout our lives.

VI

———❈———

WILL YOU STILL
NEED YOU?

A light he was to no one but himself.

—Robert Frost

Finding New Ways of Seeing Time Passing. Photo by and courtesy of Angela Browne-Miller.

Story #36

Stanton Q., Age 89

Stanton Q. is an 89-year-old man who asked that his son speak for him to do this interview. His son, James Q. is 64. Stanton Q. lives in a nursing home, is frail and leaves his bed very rarely. Yet when Stanton Q. heard about this study, he wanted to be interviewed, if his son could do the talking for him. James Q., his son, explains that he knows his father very well, that they are very close, and that he has talked with his father "about just about everything there is to talk about."

Stanton Q. says (through James Q.) that he does not worry about getting older, that he is "already old. So old is already here." This is an advantage, James Q. says Stanton Q. says, as this "helps stop the worrying about aging." When asked to say more about this comment, James replies that, "Well, some of it was my worrying, you know, wondering how much more difficult could my father's aging process get...for him...well for him and for the people who love him."

When we pointed out that James Q. was speaking for himself here, James Q. said he knew this, and he really was also talking for his father, as his father had "also been wondering how hard his aging process could get. Could it be more frightening, more painful, more of a stress for himself and for his kids?...We were scared a few times. My Dad started to say 'maybe I just should end this whole thing right now.'" At this time, there is what James Q. describes as "a sort of accepting of the whole thing, a sort of saying that this is the way it is, and that is that. But it took years getting here, to this way of being with all this. Acceptance. . . . Before now, we all tried to fight my dad's aging. We were very angry about it, even my dad was. Now we're all in a better place. There is a sort of spiritual approach to it all that took us a while to get to."

Ida J., Age 84

Ida J. is an 84-year-old married female. She has three adult children. She has seven grandchildren and one great grandchild. She has been married to the same man for 60 years. She and her husband have lived in the same house for 55 years. Although she once worked as a nurse, she has been retired for some 25 years.

Ida J. thinks that "I'm already old! I've been old for a while. Getting older is just part of what I do now. I get older every day." The interesting thing about Ida J. is that instead of talking about what she considers old, she talks about what she considers young. She will refer to some one in his 60s as "young," or some one in her 50s as "very young."

Ida J. says she spends most of her time watching TV, and reading. She likes being older because now people come visit her "and I don't have to go anywhere." She has faced several "problems of being older" such as falling and breaking bones, and dealing with what the doctors tell her is brain mass shrinkage that can cause memory loss or dementia, so she "has to take pills." Ida J. says this scares her a bit, but she doesn't really feel the effects of it. She says she is now more upset over the fact that she is "a full two inches shorter than I used to be. On a good day, I was five feet tall. Not any more. I may be getting older, but does getting shorter have anything to do with getting older?"

Ida J. says that her children do not take part in taking care of her or of her husband. But, she says proudly, does have an adult grandson that visits once a week and helps with things around the house that they can no longer do, such as trimming foliage in the yard, "fixing things," and so on. "But his company is even better than his help."

Ida J. worries a great deal about being alone, and is "very afraid of what might happen" if her husband dies. She chooses not to expand on this particular subject. Ida J. says most of her friends "have already passed away." She has indeed lost a majority of her friends in the past 10 years. She still has a few "girlfriends" that she talks to on the phone, but does not visit in person as much she used to, because it is "much harder now for all of us to travel." Ida J.'s sister is deceased but her younger brother, who is 78, is alive. For Ida J., this is "some comfort, a great comfort."

Story #38

Louis E., Age 87

Louis E. is an 87-year-old married man. He has three children, five grand-children, and two great grandchildren. He has been married to his wife for 67 years. Louis E. served in the military and fought in World War II. He then became an insurance salesman, a job from which he has been retired for many years.

Louis E. says he knows he's old, but "that doesn't stop me from doing what I want." He still climbs onto the roof and cleans the gutters regard-less of the fact that he has had three heart attacks (all of which occurred in his 70s), and has recently developed vertigo. Louis E. takes pride in being a "competent person. I can drive, I can do almost everything you can do, and I have over 60 years on you," he says. Louis E. says he is "not the type to get concerned about getting older....I don't think about it. It doesn't concern me."

What does concern Louis E. is what will happen if his wife "passes" be-fore he does. He thinks he "won't last longer than 24 hours without her." He chooses not to discuss this any further. Louis E. dislikes the fact that his children live so very far away, but he feels that he doesn't "need their help anyway. We're just fine without them."

Louis E. used to "wake up at 4 am every morning and meet a group of friends at the coffee shop for coffee at 5 am." He explains that when the group started it was with 10 men, and now there are only three of them left. Only two of them are healthy enough to make it out for breakfast now.

Louis E. and his wife have been "living frugally our whole lives and live the same way now." His retirement and their social security is what they live on and "we're perfectly fine doing just that." Louis is quite proud of this.

Derrick G., Age 80

Derrick G. is an 80-year-old man, living alone. He says he once long ago had a wife but that "that marriage did not work out, so I've been alone ever since. No kids." Derrick G. reports that he does "not mind this, and actually I like my time to myself, because I am a painter, and I need my time and room to work." His small apartment is filled with art supplies, old easels, and his artwork, largely oil paintings, some in process, some complete and framed and hanging on the walls.

Derrick G. tells a story of a life in what he calls "a suit, walking the halls of corporate America, until I was finally free." When Derrick G. retired, he figured that between his social security, his retirement investments, and what he could sell his paintings for, he "would be set." However, financial stress has become a way of life for Derrick G. His savings has gone more rapidly than he had expected. In fact, he had expected that he would use only the interest on his savings, however this has not been the case. Derrick G. does sell his artwork from time to time, and is highly regarded in local art circles, however the income he had expected from his "profession as a painter" has not been anywhere near what he thought it would be.

Derrick G. is proud of the fact that he lives alone, still works at his age, and is independent. He says, "I do not want to need anybody. This is when you get into trouble, because if you need people and then they are not there for you, you get hurt." When asked what he feels about the aging process, he replies, "Well, I would have preferred to never get old, but if I have to, then I think my state of mind is a good one for aging." (When this interviewer offered to help Derrick G. carry a heavy laundry bag, Derrick G. insisted sternly that he needed no help.)

Story #40

Lisa Lynn C., Age 77

Lisa Lynn C. is 77 years old. She lives alone, and has been living alone since she lost her husband 12 years ago. Lisa Lynn C. has two children and four grandchildren, who live nearby. "Well not too nearby, they live 50 miles away, a comfortable distance I always say. This way they can't drop in on me, but when I need them, they can get here pretty fast. They also can't expect us to babysit their kids. Ha!"

Lisa Lynn C. recalls the time after she lost her husband: "He was sick for a couple years, so I had some time to get ready. But no matter how ready I thought I was, it hit me very hard, losing him. For a while I just wanted to die.... It was bad.... Then I realized I had a lot of years ahead of me. At first this was awful...after a while this was good."

Lisa Lynn C. lives on "very little a month. We didn't have much and spent a lot of it when my husband Fred was sick. But we knew how to live on next to nothing, and I still know this." Lisa Lynn C. says she is not worried about her Social Security and Medicare "running out" because she is "used to counting on these things. I just know they will always be here for me." Lisa Lynn C. adds, "I don't have a lot of money and don't have a lot of things, but just want to be here, in my apartment, as long as I can, with little things from my whole life all around me.... Anyway, this could be a very long time, you know. I may be around another 20 years plus some."

"What do I do with my time, well I just watch television and take walks and talk to my cat," Lisa Lynn C. says. She adds. "I try to keep busy so I won't be too lonely. I don't like empty time too much, this is when I get sad. I don't want to feel sad the rest of my life. If I do, then what am I still doing here? If I let myself, I could get pretty darn sad about having no more real friends or my husband around. . . . But instead I make myself like my life. This isn't really very different from what other people of other ages do, is it? We make ourselves accept what happens when we cannot change it."

Commentary

This sixth set of stories includes interviews with persons whose ages range from 77 to 89. Here we feel the immediacy of growing older. Now aging is ever more front and center, there is no way to deny its reality. Here coping with aging, making sense out of aging, and feeling positive about aging, not only assist in the process but also can have positive effects on mental and physical health while aging. Also quite apparent is that many if not most aging persons do best when they have a close (especially somewhat close in age) personal companion in their lives. Some can add to, enhance, or even replace this close personal companionship with a personal activity, hobby, avocation to which they are dedicated.

We see in the comments of these interviewees that there is an acceptance of having aged, and of growing older and older. Being alive to grow old is of value. Being somewhat comfortable in life, or at least finding a modicum of comfort in life, is also valuable, and can soothe and even enhance the aging process. What meaning in life can be found by looking back on one's life is valuable. What meaning in life can be found by looking at one's life as it is in the present is also valuable.

With the end of life being closer and perhaps within sight, some persons at these ages are acutely aware of time passing. More than this, when losing friends to old age or for other reasons, while undergoing aging one self, brings the reality of end of life into focus. Now the end, or at least some one's end of life, is right before us. The time of one's life is appreciated all the more now. Life is appreciated all the more now. So is one's ability to function.

26

—⚬⚬⚬—

Youth for Sale: The Distraction of Anti-Aging Consumption

"55? Oh, you're a baby still. I've got 30 years on you. That's a whole adulthood. So, you've got nothing on me, except for youth," the 85-year-old said.

Youth? Yes, youth. We live in a society that places great value on youth, and on looking young, acting young, thinking young—whether this be 20 or 30 or 40. Youth itself is sold, as an image, as a state of mind. There are doctors who will work on your face and body—surgically—to make you look younger, There are drugs that will make you feel, at least temporarily, young and high. We want it, we have to have it, we crave it—youth. Youth is a commodity that appears to be something we can buy. But we cannot really pay to stop the clock—and then to turn it back. Actual time—and the stopping of time—has no price and cannot be bought. Yet it is common for people to resist even any degree of aging if they can find a way or an approximate way to feel that they are doing this. (How many people do you know who lie about their ages? And why?)

Craving youth is, in some ways, similar to just about all craving of anything else we want a great deal or perhaps are addicted to (a concept we return to below). We are, after all, consuming animals—great consumers. So much of our cultural overlay is dedicated to the buying and selling and feeding of states of mind, and to the things that go with these states of mind, to the consumer—and to fueling the ever present and ever growing compulsion to buy experiences, and things, things, things. We are bombarded by advertisements to buy buy buy anything and everything, and to eat eat eat food, and to drug drug drug ourselves.

Is overconsumption, what is frequently driven by addiction to these states of mind and these things, merely an individual malady, or is it our human species-generated response to our own environmental stimulation of ourselves to consume, consume, consume? And is this drive to over demand, to over want, to over consume youth part of the larger overconsumption picture—buy buy buy, want want want, think-we-need think-we-need think-we-need, crave crave crave? It may be that we carry some sort of biological imperative, programming to want to remain young and healthy—or think we want to. In fact, the latter, the desire to be "healthy," is most likely the underlying drive. And this is not surprising, as survival does involve remaining healthy and therefore appearing healthy—to would be (or to would have been) mates. These desires are not necessarily superficial instincts. Of course we want to be at least somewhat healthy when we are young and then to stay healthy as we grow older.

However, health itself does not stop all aging. It may slow the emerging and ongoing effects and signs of aging, but it will not stop these things all together. Still, we may be confusing health with youth. Can it be that we are an animal that cannot clearly distinguish between being healthy and simply being young? Are we confusing the signs of youth with those of health? Attractiveness can be confusing. Its real messages can be blurred by desire in the now being combined with the ancient instinct we carry to drive us to act on feeling desire and then to act on desire in the now.

Perhaps we are programmed to seek health and what appears to be health in youth, to not see aging as desirable. The programmed robot within us rises, run by automatic biological programming mechanisms. The robot within us is at once the prison and the prisoner of our lives. Meet the biological robot: You, me, everyone. And this robot is programmed to look away from the positive side of aging. The robot is addicted to being young, forever young—or what it feels youth to be.

Responding to this programming, this drive to be forever young, to decry aging, we must see what our programming is telling us, and how it is now misinforming us. What if we were programmed to believe being old is desirable? Attractive? Can we be programmed to believe this? What would this look like on a population level? We programmed robots can rebel! We can see, understand, respond to, and experience our aging processes entirely differently. We can completely rethink the meaning of our aging, and thereby the psychology of our aging.

Where do we start? We start with ourselves.

27

---❧❧❧---

Thinking Positive: Prescription for Aging Well?

We know there is no magic pill, no medicine that can stop the clock. Time does pass. Nothing changes this. However, it turns out that good attitude is good medicine, especially good preventative medicine. It has become clear to many individuals doing the aging, as well as to many scientists researching the aging, that thinking in a positive way about aging while aging can be a life extender. Estimates are that at least seven and a half years can be added to your life just by thinking positively. (This effect is even true after controlling for gender, age, income, social isolation, and general health.) This is because the way we see our aging processes has a great deal to do with how we experience aging. Our feelings about growing older can be more (rather than less) positive and then can render the experience of growing older more (rather than less) positive. The idea that how long we live can be affected so powerfully by something that appears so simple is finally coming of age.

What is perhaps more astounding is that thinking positively about aging (long before experiencing middle age and older age) while young also positively and even more powerfully effects longevity. Thinking ahead this way can have powerful future as well as present time effects. Now that we know this, we may want to model positive views of the aging process to young people, to contribute to their well being far in the future when they find themselves aging. A new mind set regarding aging can spread throughout the population. But do we know aging well enough to model a true understanding of what aging is? And how do we show the young how rich the aging process can be? We never know for sure exactly what our aging processes hold for us. Outcomes of the aging process cannot be perfectly predicted in terms of longevity and quality of life. Yet it is quite clear that our aging process is made more positive when guided by positive attitude regarding all aging: aging in the present time; aging in the future; aging in ourselves; aging in others.

Like a special medicine, potent, elixir, optimism—positive attitude combined with hope—contributes to survival. Optimism markedly lowers stress levels, definitely increases the will to live, and powerfully encourages positive health practices, even in situations that are indeed stressful. Optimism is essential to survival and also to well-being while surviving. People who are optimistic not only experience less stress and not only are generally healthier, they are also more productive, have stronger relationships, see problems they experience as the result of influences outside themselves rather than blaming themselves, engage in positive self-talk, are less bothered by failure, and are more pleased with success. These are great reasons for being optimistic.

Feeling needed, or at least useful, is also a major factor in quality of life while aging and longevity. Feeling useful also helps to make the aging process a positive experience. In fact, older persons who rate their own usefulness highly are less likely to suffer from chronic disease. Those who do not feel useful tend to show higher rates of chronic illness and earlier death rates. And we have only just begun to see how very important feeling useful is in the aging process.

Being engaged in positive relationships, at least one positive relationship, can also have a distinctly positive effect on health and longevity in older age. A positive relationship can bring with it positive biochemical effects in the body. These effects are health promoting, stress reducing, and identity reinforcing. Being involved in a healthy relationship as one ages is valuable when that relationship is a close personal positive relationship, one that is indeed healthy as this relationship becomes a source of positive feedback and also of social support.

Social support itself can have positive health effects and contribute to longevity. Older persons who rarely participate in social activities age more rapidly in several ways, including along the dimension of muscular function decline. Some claim that those who attend religious services, (they are a form of social event), live significantly longer than those who do not. It is not clear whether this particular effect is the result of regular engagement in social activity or regular engagement in a psychologically fulfilling activity, or both.

Of course some of the value of social support is simply that it is helpful and convenient. Help planning appointments, transportation, shopping, communications with the outside world, is a powerful plus in having social support. However, social support is also a stress reducer and in this respect has positive biochemical effects on the body. Most importantly, social support and social engagement as one ages tells the mind and body that the self is still needed. People want to see me, people may even need to see me, I am still needed.

With one's immune and other biological systems being fortified by optimism, feeling useful, positive relationships, and positive social support in older age, it is all the more certain that the health of the elderly is profoundly sensitive, flexible, and responsive to some very simple adjustments. Say yes when you hear the silent question, *will you still need me?*, say yes to yourself and see that you can want *to still need yourself.*

28

⚬⚬⚬

Longevity, Spirit, and
Quality of Life

A great deal of emphasis is placed, by the media and by society in general, on maintaining one's youth. An unspoken attitude toward being old floats in the social atmosphere, like an unacknowledged elephant in the room reflects a whispering personal concern regarding one's own growing old, a social pressure, and biological programming. The general reaction to aging is to quite naturally respond to it with underlying and even surface negativity and fear of various sorts. Yet there are many aspects of aging that are distinctly positive. For example, there is having had more experience in life—yes, experience itself. Time growing older allows for gaining more experience in a lifetime. There is also maturity, something gained over time. There is also the combination of experience and maturity, which can give older people deeper insights into life, its events, its ups and downs.

Additionally, with growing older there is the opportunity to develop or regain, whether through religion or independent of religion, a greater sense of self, or spirit, or spirituality, and of spiritual and or emotional priorities, that have great meaning to the individual. The positive influence on one's aging process of a personal world view or spirituality (whether this be religious or another form of worldview) cannot be emphasized enough. Such a worldview offers meaning, organization, purpose in life, and thereby contributes to ongoing identity and motivation as well as general well-being, optimism, and general health.

Meaning in life contributes greatly to well-being. This meaning in life is very personal. What your life means to you is up to you. No one can decide for you what your life means. No one can tell you what sounds good to you. Nevertheless, it is important that each of us finds something or things about our lives that give us a sense of meaning. We rarely talk about meaning itself. Meaning is actually a state of mind. What one person finds to have meaning may not be what another finds to have meaning, and in fact may not even have been seen by another person. Finding, defining, meaning in life is central to good mental health.

With meaning in life, and the motivation to be engaged in one's own life this brings, mental and physical health can be enhanced. Is it clear that definitions and qualities of mental and physical health in older ages are different from what these are for the young. Among other things, when it comes to aging persons' mental and physical health, less is taken for granted, less is expected perhaps. However mental and physical health as we age matters all the more then, or at least as much as it does when we are young. Where healthy attitudes and lifestyles are already in place, or even just started in old age, there is great advantage in terms of longevity and quality of life as one lives longer.

Meaning and motivation in life can impact one's health on many levels. For example, years can be added to one's life by making simple behavioral or lifestyle changes including lowering blood pressure, which can add at least some four years to the life span; lowering cholesterol, which can add at least four years to the life span; maintaining a healthy weight, which can add at least three years to the life span; exercising regularly, which can add at least three years to the life span; and not smoking, which can add at least 14 years to the life span.

Beyond the decision never to smoke (or to stop smoking where one has smoked), exercise is one of the greatest contributions to extended life span with quality of life in that life span. Although this is rather obvious, it is clear that many people are slow to start a regular exercise regimen. However, once they build this in, the exercise regimen can be continued throughout life. It is such a great idea to always be using your muscles, to always be making these muscles stronger and more efficient. Far too much of the frailty seen in old age comes with lack of use of the muscles.

It is never too late to change the curve of your own life span and quality of life. You can always start today to turn things around, to get your body working smoothly. Also note that activity itself helps to ward off disease. Exercise helps ward off several diseases common in old age and in earlier stages of life as well: stroke, heart disease, type 2 diabetes—by lowering cholesterol levels, controlling blood pressure, preventing hardening of the arteries, and helping maintain a healthy weight. Exercise also helps to control arthritis pain and blood sugar levels, osteoporosis, insomnia, and even constipation.

The basic exercise categories are all quite important in working to increase life span and quality of life: aerobic exercise, muscular conditioning (strength training), stretching exercises, balance exercises, and endurance exercises. Always talk to your doctor before jumping into exercise if you have not already been exercising. First and foremost, always be safe while you exercise. And also key is enjoyment of exercise (although not to the sacrificing of safety.) The enjoyment of exercise is as important as the above benefits. Enjoyment of activities is a large part of enjoying life, which is a large part of longevity and quality of life itself. Longevity and quality of life do not necessarily or always come together, but can combine to add positive factors to the aging experience.

There is no magic pill to prevent or stop aging. Yes, modern science is working on such things, however we are not there yet, if we will ever be there. However, with new compounds on the horizon, we can look forward to the emergence of anti-aging "medicines" such as "rapamycin," which is known for extending the life span of mice. Of course, humans are not mice and may have other responses to this drug. Ongoing testing is necessary. Also note that human growth hormones have been shown to reduce frailty in the elderly. And, already we are finding that drugs used for some health problems may have other benefits as we age. For example, cholesterol reducing statin drugs taken to reduce cholesterol may have the added positive effect of helping to prevent dementia.

All this being said, it is nevertheless the case that some of the most simple changes in lifestyle can alter the aging curve in significantly positive ways. Simply put, a few simple parts of life can add both time and quality to a life span:

- thinking positively, optimism, feeling useful, finding meaning
- social activities, having at least one positive personal relationship
- moderate appropriate exercise and reduced caloric intake
- playing games of strategy

Adding these areas into a life at any point in time can shift the curve of aging to a much slower pace, and shift the quality of life to a much more positive range. The message here is that *you must still need you*, and take what steps you can take to respect and address this need.

29

———∞∞∞———

Addiction to Reality

Try turning back the hands of time. It just doesn't work. Aging involves changes. There is no way around this. If nothing else, we are adding a year to our ages each year we live. However, many want to resist even that degree of change. (How many people do you know who lie about their ages?) We are both changing in general, and also changing the way we see our selves and life itself.

We not only resist aging, we even become stubborn about leaving, even somewhat addicted to, realities that must change as we age. This addiction to the desire to stay young is a pattern of resistance to aging. "I want that phase of life back." "I want that time of my life back." "I want that me back." "I want that body back." "I want that face back." Our perceptions of our realities, our ways of being, all our behaviors, carry elements of the habitual.

We spend so many years forming our identities. Just when we get who we are straight, we realize we've changed. We depend upon the habits we form. We identify with these habits. When we have to see that old definitions of ourselves need modification as we grow older, we may even resist adapting our identities to new circumstances.

We are inherently programmed to resist many forms of change, to become addicted to something and to stay that way. And for good reason. This is how our biological machine (made up of our brain and our body) is designed to work. In fact, we as biological machines are not wired to find most change easy for us. Instead, we are wired to be addicted: to the way things are; to what we have come to do repeatedly; and to what we have come to believe is our reality, even our identity in our reality.

We (both as individuals and as a population) tend to try to preserve the status quo. Living, even surviving, relies on our very reliance on life-protecting and life-sustaining patterns. Yet, this valuable susceptibility to programming, an ability we have evolved over a long period of time, and passed from generation to generation via tradition and culture and even via genetic mechanisms, can and has run awry. The very characteristic that helps us survive, even ensures our survival, can make the aging process difficult for us.

This is our most basic, ever present and always underlying, susceptibility to the process of what I describe as *pattern-addiction*. Surely this is an essential life-protecting function, yet it is one that now surely too frequently does run awry, morphing into a sort of self-induced or self-allowed brainwashing. *Understanding the natural pattern addiction functions we carry within us is essential to our clearly understanding the difficult time we have leaving ages and times of life that are moving into the past.* And in fact we do have such a difficult time with changes that we tend to deny these are taking place.

Change can feel like losing the reality to which we are hugely attached and perhaps upon which we are entirely dependent—the only reality we feel we know, the only thing we feel we are. In essence, growing older does call for breaking an addiction to past definitions of ourselves. *Our identities have to further develop, not stay the same.*

We are all wired to form habits and addictions. The problem is, we are also all wired to form addictions to behaviors our brains tell us to be addicted to. The SELF falls prey to the underlying coding or wiring to be addicted to patterns and to be addicted to being addicted to patterns. Therefore, when we want to break an addiction to a past definition of self, we have to rewire the SELF. Move over old self, make room for the new person, older, wiser, and moving on. (I have explained this concept, pattern addiction—natural addiction to patterns—more fully in my book, *Rewire Your Self to Break Habits and Addictions*.)

30

You Can Make It Through

You have been born, you have walked your first steps. You likely had a first day of school, had a favorite pet, became an adolescent, fell in love for the first time, broke up with your first boy friend or girl friend, finished school, left home, got hired, and or maybe have been laid off or fired, married, maybe divorced, perhaps have mourned the death of a family member or friend, or have experienced some other important life events and changes. Certainly some but not all of these events are considered difficult experiences. Perhaps some are considered okay or even joyous experiences. Many of these events are considered natural parts of life.

Changes and transitions, including aging, are part of life. Yet we have a difficult time with many of these, including aging. In fact, even positive events such as graduating from high school can be tearful events. So many changes and transitions feel like endings. And coming to the end of something can bring with it parting anxieties, even when an ending may be good or positive. The ending itself, the transition out of a state or phase of life, the closing of a cycle, can bring with it feelings of loss. In fact, for many people, major endings such as divorces and job losses feel somewhat like dying. In fact, while these and other intense endings are not actual dyings, these can nevertheless bring with them feelings of loss and grief, plus anxiety regarding separation from a previous reality, and a form of "separation anxiety" itself.

It should come as no surprise that aging can bring with it what I have come to call an *end of phase anxiety*, plus the sense of loss and grief that we may find in other closings and transitional events. Sometimes this end of phase anxiety is continuous, as it appears every day it is a deeper movement into the passage away from youth. However, no one tells us in advance that aging might for some people feel like this, at least once during the aging process, if not every day. In fact, there are very few forms of formal assistance with the aging process. Aging just "happens" to most people. It is a sort of sink or swim experience, something we sometimes do as if "flying without wings" or at least without a compass. Where are we going when we age? What direction are we taking? How much say can we have in the process of getting older? How will we know for certain whether anyone will still need or want us tomorrow?

Many people feel that there is rather little ongoing guidance available to us regarding aging. Many do not access, or perhaps do not find personally accessible, what various religions and philosophies have to say regarding aging. Whether or not one accesses these resources, we all would do well to allow ourselves to fully understand and appreciate—even relish and cherish—the cycles of life, including aging. Essentially, everything has a beginning, a middle, and an end. And essentially, growing older is movement through time away from one's birth. This life has a first part or beginning. This life has a middle. This life has a latter part or ending. Yet, we can observe that as the average life span is extending, the end of this life is on average pushed out later and later in time away from birth. The life cycle is extending.

This allows for an ever growing number of what I like to call *adventures in the life cycle*. Sure, there are bumps in the road. Sure, portions of the trip can be challenging to say the least. Still, knowing what it is we are traveling, and what the process we are living through is, does help. This is especially true as we navigate that great frontier, aging.

Certainly we feel changes and transitions. Frequently these are growing pains. Sometimes these are the pains of not growing while needing to. Sometimes this is resistance to transitions such as aging, resistance that in itself makes these transitions all the more challenging. Some of the most challenging transitions do lead people to say, "It feels like I am dying or something." Again, yes, these are closings, endings of cycles or passages in life. Any ending, as an ending, is always a transitional experience. Any ending can be for at least some people somewhat unsettling, even disturbing, frightening, painful—when we can not see this particular ending as otherwise. However, we can learn how to recognize what we think of as painful experiences as transitional events and we can learn to use these experiences well. Look back on your life. Think of the many experiences you found difficult or painful as they were happening and later saw as rough yes, yet perhaps also as a source of motivation, learning and maybe even inspiration, learning, perhaps even hope and strength.

Pain is more than just a four letter word. Pain is a sensation that hurts, either emotionally or physically or both. Anyone who has experienced intense pain knows that the *sensation of pain* is real, about as real as any experience we ever encounter. Pain cannot be denied. However, pain itself can be understood differently, reframed to help *travel the painful sensations into higher understandings and awarenesses*.

Those readers who have given birth to babies may know the feeling of labor pains—of pain cycling in and out, of traveling through layers or rings of pain that quicken over time until a baby is born. Think of any transitional process, including aging, as giving birth to your further or new self, and any accompanying emotional and or physical pain as transitional labor pain. Now there is a direction to the pain, and an outcome to the process. This outcome is a birth into a new reality: your new next phases of life and new ways of seeing life. Even as we age, there are opportunities for new ways of seeing our lives.

Again, not all endings or passages to new phases are painful or traumatic. Every day begins and ends, cycles through day and night. Every breath you take begins and ends, cycles through an inhale-exhale process. Everything you do has a cycle to it. We tend to move right through many endings and beginnings, too busy to realize that we have just survived one of an infinite number of transitions we undergo every single day. (We wake up, we go to sleep. We breathe in, we breathe out. And so on.) We also tend to pay little attention to the many other, and the many far larger, cycles we are living within and around. I have included a diagram on page 195 that depicts this reality—that suggests that we live in and around cycles, and within larger and smaller cycles within cycles within cycles within cycles.

So we do know that we travel, or traverse, many large and small transitions in our lifetimes, so many that we cannot possibly notice each and every one of these. We may not feel we have time to consciously navigate every single transition we undergo every single minute of our lives. However, we can incorporate increased awareness of consciousness into any activity we want to be more aware of. For example, we can engage in more conscious breathing, more conscious eating, more conscious relating—more conscious behavior. This is possible on all fronts. So then is conscious aging. It is here, in this state of paying attention to the processes we are living out, and living through that we can make the most of these processes, including the aging process.

Aging is full of transitions. And, transition itself is the opportunity to recognize and develop new parts of the self, to even stimulate pathways in the brain not yet used, or rarely so far used, or long ago used. *A great deal of energy is locked up in the transitions of our lives. And this energy is our energy.*

We can indeed *harvest* our transitions through the phases or stages of our lives, If you, reader, are thinking about this right now, as you read, consider the possibility that your harvest can be as abundant as you wish it to be. You can learn as much as you choose to from most anything you undergo, including aging. You can harvest a strengthened self from the process of transition. Even if the transition is one of the more challenging passages you undergo during your life—a troubled divorce or other family breakup; a major downturn in financial, career, health or social status; a physical disaster of some sort; or aging itself—*you can transform the process as you experience it.* Again, you can transform your experience of the process—transform it from merely a tough or troubling ordeal, merely an unpleasant experience through which you seem to be aimlessly and hopelessly tumbling, into a *profound personal experience.* You can transform yourself in the process. Aging is therefore a great opportunity.

Again, this is not to deny any pain that may be experienced. We all know pain, some of us more directly and intensely than others. Pain cannot be denied and it is unfair to deny the reality of another's pain simply because we are not feeling it. Pain is present in many intense experiences. Given that pain is present, why not put the *experience of pain* to work? Why not allow the pain to be useful in deepening the self, the awareness, the knowledge of the self of the person experiencing the pain (either directly—or indirectly by witnessing or sensing it).

Pain does far more than just hurt. Both emotional and physical pain call our attention to the fact that something is taking place. Pain can be a sign of change, or of need for change, or for a change in understanding of what is taking place. While change can seem to and can actually hurt, so can not changing when change is needed. We may be stuck and need to move through a situation—go into what I call *transit mode*—or we may be moving through the situation and register the experience as painful. When we are stuck, we may need to resolve the pressure or stuck sensation by consciously entering into, or deeper into, a conscious transition process, a purposeful transit mode.

Whether it be emotional or physical, pain can be part of, or transformed into something which is part of, an initiation into a next phase, a new way of seeing the world, a new way of seeing life. A lot of energy is contained in pain. Therefore, pain can be fuel for a change in awareness, when pain is understood this way. On some level we are aware of this. Yet, few people consciously prepare for the initiations the steps of life bring us. This is because we tend to be avoidant of, or even afraid of, great changes, great transitions, and especially seemingly great unknowns such as aging can be. So we do not consciously plan for changes and transitions, except to buy insurance, write wills, and pray for some kind of salvation or direction.

Drawing closer in time (chronologically) to the end of one's life span, end of life awareness emerges. The ability to accept and even embrace this time in one's life can be learned. Guidance is available. Aging can be a profound psychological journey, a spiritual journey, a journey of the spirit. Even where there has not been a deepening of self prior to growing older, there can be one now, with every moment of your aging—no matter what your age.

VII

EXPERIENCING AGING IN NEW WAYS

The mind that is wise mourns less for what age takes away, than what it leaves behind.

—William Wordsworth

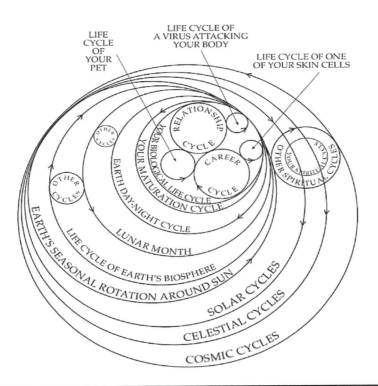

Cycles within Cycles within Cycles. Illustration by and courtesy of Angela Browne-Miller.

31

Toward a New Paradigm for Aging

The issues discussed herein touch each and every one of us in our own families and communities. Add to this that these same issues touch the growing population of aging persons around the globe. That this world-wide population of older persons is growing at a remarkable rate has to be seen for its impact on each individual who is, or will someday be, either old, older, or growing older. As the human population ages, and birthrates begin to drop, a host of issues are emerging. For example, it has become clear that where birthrates may drop, workforces may eventually shrink. Where life spans may extend while birthrates drop and future workforces shrink, we face not only a changing ratio of young to old (fewer younger persons, more older persons), but also a changing ratio of job seeking workers to older persons who may no longer work, even where they want to work (fewer younger workers, more older persons).

Whole economies of whole nations will face the challenges posed by increasing numbers of aging persons, whether or not their own birthrates will rapidly and radically drop. On a societal, national and global level, we have to pay close attention to these developments to best navigate the changing age structure of the human population. These are human species-wide issues, and yet these are also intensely personal (individual human being), issues. We are being pressed to see aging in new ways, to understand what it means to have a growing aging population, and also to understand what it means to be growing older as an individual.

Aging is an equal opportunity condition. Aging happens. There is no magic bullet to stop time from progressing. It may be that, as we grow older, we see this more and more, as if a distant reality is now coming into full view. Still, as much a given as aging is, the views we hold on aging, our ways of seeing aging, do affect us as we age. Understanding what aging is, what happens to us physically as we age, how to take care of ourselves as we age, are essential contributors to aging with awareness. Aging is a profound opportunity—if we have the opportunity to see it that way.

As one interviewee put it, "Aging is a stressful part of life if you are not ready for it, if you are not adequately prepared for it, or if the misfortune of poor health strikes you to the point you cannot recover. Otherwise, aging may become one of life's richest experiences as one has the time and hopefully the resources, at least some little bit of resources, to truly enjoy life. But enjoying life is not really about money, I can sit here in the garden and see so much beauty. It's being able to know there is beauty in the world, no matter how hard aging is. That's what makes being in the world so worth it."

"Being able to know there is beauty in the world . . ." this interviewee emphasizes. What an important part of adapting well to, and successfully navigating the process of, one's own aging. And yet there are other feelings about aging not so respecting of its expanding possibilities and great significance. Perceptions of aging are too often dependent upon so much more than our own internal points of view. Our experience of aging is—at least in part—a *construction,* something made up of what we indirectly hear being said about, and what we are directly being told about, aging. Too much of aging is something the world around us tells us is taking place, or will take place as we grow old. Too much of aging is what the world around us tells us aging feels like, or will feel like. *The experience of aging is indeed a social construction.* It may even be that the barrage of aging-related social messages we receive can be not only mildly inaccurate but also quite distorting of our experiences of aging. For example, these messages can reach into us and convince us that aging is a process in which we definitely decline in function and usefulness. This is a common belief regarding aging. Yet this perception is not necessarily the case, and is quite frequently wrong. Declines in a sense of one's mental function and general usefulness, while sometimes occurring, are quite frequently states of mind, or products of social isolation or other conditions outside—not internal, not inside—the individual that can be changed.

So much of deep seated and only partially acknowledged negativity and fear surrounding aging is constructed, built into us. We may take this flawed social construction of aging into us, and even believe in it. We may be blocked from seeing our own and others' aging as an important passage in life, even a rich experience, something to be respected and treated as special. We may hear or sense social messages saying that the stages of life past the age of 50 are less intricate and less critical than the stages of childhood and adolescence—although there are many stages of life over 50 and over 60, 70, 80, 90, and even 100 that can be understood in as great detail as are the stages of children's lives!

That there are countless powerful misperceptions regarding aging is not surprising as just about everything around us pulls attention to, as well as social support for, the development and progress of young people rather than pulling attention and support for the development and progress of older persons. Resources are directed toward the young and away from us as we age. This is not to say that the young should not have access to resources and that the young do not need what these resources can offer. Rather this is to say that those growing old can be and are still valuable members of our population. They should be encouraged to be, and resources should indeed be focused upon them being, valuable and contributing members of our population.

Clearly one's personal as well as social and cultural identity can continue to evolve, and even to continue to emerge well into later life, in fact, throughout life. Aging can be a gift, the gift of time, time to know oneself, time to deepen one's knowledge of oneself, time to search for more knowledge of oneself, or perhaps time to know oneself for the first time. Ultimately, whether *you will still need you* will be a major determinant of the course and outcome of your aging process.

We can apply the profound words of Helen Keller, "Life is either a great adventure or nothing." While every day of life is an adventure, every day of aging is a special sort of adventure. Here, in this precious phase of our lives, we are able to see ourselves moment by moment, as we age over time. We are able to witness the essence of ourselves as we let go of self-definitions we held when we were younger. We are able to free ourselves of limiting societal definitions regarding this time of our lives we call aging. Free to age as we choose to see our own aging, we can affect not only our own individual aging processes, but those of the human population. Transforming aging to a new model, a new paradigm for aging, begins with each of us.

32

A New Adventure
in the Life Cycle

Aging can be a whole new adventure in the life cycle. We can celebrate this time in our own and others' lives. We can make the aging process mean so much more to ourselves and to the world around us. We can give the aging process voice, let it speak to us, and show us what aging can be.

A complete overhaul of the way we see aging is already under way. New attitudes toward one's own and others' aging are emerging. Caring about health as we age, purpose and meaning in life as we age, fulfillment as we age, even work as we age, is on the increase. We see older people exercising virtually everywhere we look. We find groups of older persons painting, traveling, studying, returning to school, taking on second and even third careers, and reaching out for deepening experiences as they seek greater meaning in their lives and in their aging processes.

With ever more frequency, we find older persons wanting (and also needing) to find employment yet unable to find it. Although age discrimination is increasingly prevented, there is an unspoken bias against older persons when they seek to retain their own jobs, when they apply for new jobs, and when they take up new professions "later in life." While the workforce is teeming with younger, and more recently educated with more up-to-date training, adults in line for jobs and promotions, older persons do compete for work where they can. Still this can be quite difficult, as the doors of opportunity for older workers can be closed. This can be a daunting, discouraging, even demoralizing situation. Yet, this situation need not be the only option. A new model of the older worker can be brought forward.

Recall the old adage, "when one door closes, another opens." And here it is: when one door to one opportunity closes, another can indeed be opened. When the workforce appears to close to aging persons, another door can be opened. Older persons can generate a great new wave of entrepreneurialism—*elder entrepreneurialism*. Older persons can form a new economic pool of demand for their ideas, services, and products. They can also form a new economic pool of supply of the ideas, services and products they can generate. Let's call this the *elder economy* and make every effort to realize its power. Once the economic and creative power of those growing older is fully recognized by those growing older, this can be a significant shift in our experiences and understandings of aging. This shift must come from the elder population itself. The fuel for this monetizing—or at least giving economic value to—the ideas, creativity, wisdom, and work of this precious resource, the elder population, has to come from within that population. Put that elder ingenuity and wisdom to work!

33

———⊗⊗⊗———

Recommendations for an Emerging Social Force: Older People and Those Who Will One Day Be Older People

In today's world, growing up and growing older and then older is an intense and challenging journey containing many stages, phases, and cycles of life, each intense and challenging in its own way. This is of course a journey that can be profoundly rewarding as well. The challenges and the rewards are privately experienced by individuals and they are publicly experienced by entire populations. In these times, we are increasingly aware of the population, social, biological, environmental, and economic pressures we as members of the human species face. Our senses of self-worth are being formed against the backdrop of intense individual and population level survival pressures.

At every stage of life, the awareness of what it means to grow older is with us. While during the early stages of life and young adulthood, this awareness is somewhat vague, almost buried amidst identity formation processes, at other stages it is front and center. *The challenge is to see the central focus and central meaning of one's life emerge and then shift or expand as we move through the stages and phases of life.*

- In childhood and adolescence, aging is primarily seen as something that happens to others. We may know older persons and grandparents, we may love them very much, however we do not directly identify with their experiences of aging. *The central focus and central meaning of life here: growing up (with all the learning, testing, and exploration that involves). Forge an identity separate from one's parents and family of origin.*

- Young adults in their 20s and early 30s, such as those in Stories 2–6 (found in part one of this book), are aware of other persons' aging, although this is a rather distant reality for them. Among the priorities at this stage of life are establishing the ability to make a living, and for some, finding a mate. Establishing oneself and one's identity as an adult is also central. Being alone is an issue, however this concern regarding being alone is more focused on the desire to be "in a (primary) relationship" and not be without one, than on the concern that one may "someday end up experiencing aging alone." This aging alone possibility is out there, well into the future, for people this age, however it does not occupy much attention when the matter of simply establishing oneself as an adult is underway. And this makes sense, as this is the stage of life when the focus must be to enter adulthood, establish oneself as an adult, and then to begin to thrive as an adult. *The central focus and central meaning of life here: establishing one self as a self-sufficient adult. Forge an identity as an adult.*

- Somewhat older but still "youngish" adults, in their later 30s and early 40s, as in Stories 7 (found in part one) and 8–14 (found in part two), indicate somewhat more awareness that they will someday face older if not old age. Now the search for a mate, or the desire to form, or to maintain and fortify an already formed, family is central, as are work, career and earnings, plus children and their needs. Some of these persons are already concerned about what it might be like "to grow old alone," or to have a life partner leave them to then grow old alone. Being aware that growing old alone might be quite lonely and financially demanding, many persons in this age range find this a motivation "to be sure to have children." Now, at this stage of life, children are increasingly viewed as a form of future emotional and social, perhaps even financial, support. This is not to say that the natural drive to have children and build families is not present, this is to say that the motivation for having children is far larger than the natural drive to procreate to build a primary family. *The central focus and central meaning of life here: building and deepening the definition and meaning of one's life (family, career, other aspects of that life). Expand one's adult identity, and begin to try to protect one's future.*

- Once adults move more deeply into the "thick" of life, in their later 40s and early 50s, as in Stories 15–21 (found in part three), a range of awarenesses and concerns regarding becoming somewhat older adults are front and center. Now work, career and financial concerns, even demands, do take center stage. These share center stage along with family concerns, demands—all sorts of child, spouse, older parent, and the ever growing sandwich generation concerns, demands—plus issues such as coping with one's own health, family soundness or divorce, child rearing, and other demanding life issues. It is clear now that there are not sharp or predictable dividing lives between age ranges and age groups as per how the aging situation is seen and responded to. Stages of life are not clear cut with distinct and specific ages that match these. In this age group, especially as people enter their 50s, we find a tangled collection of life cycle issues, many positive and many challenging to say the least. At this stage of life, adult identities are more formed than they were during young adulthood, as are adult responsibilities. People's plates are full, their lives rich and quite demanding. While the matter of one's own aging is present, this matter is not the largest of the big issues and pressures being addressed now. *The central focus and central meaning of life here: ensure the survival of the next generation, as well as of the self, while meeting the complex demands and discovering the complex rewards of life. Retain the forged identity while expanding to address pressures on that identity, and while expanding to know one's self more.*

- When adults come into their later 50s and then 60s, as in Stories 22–28 (found in part four), one's own—and one's own parents'—aging is more a reality than it has been so far. People in this age range are not "old" yet, however they are noticing that their own bodies are changing, that they recover from injuries more slowly, that they are experiencing more aches and pains, that they may be more tired than they used to be. Now pressures to care for children 18 and under, and for adult age children who may be remaining entirely dependent on their parents far past the age of 18 or 20, and older parents who may or may not be able to take care of themselves, are mounting. While every age group experiences pressures related to its age, this age group is likely to be experiencing an intensification of many of the pressures experienced at earlier ages, as well as new pressures. Now their own aging is on their minds, and their own feelings of growing tired more readily are present. The complication of life pressures coming from all directions can be quite wearing and or quite strengthening in the way of the old adage, "what does not kill you makes you stronger." *The central focus and central meaning of life here: survive, even thrive, while facing the ongoing intensification of adulthood demands, (children, parents, finances, aging, etc.), Allow one's identity to grow as new phases and meanings of one's life emerge.*

- And then we come to the later 60s and 70s, as in Stories 29–35 (found in part five). A range of responses to being this age appear. Some of these differences relate to differences in retirement age, and readiness for retirement itself—both financially and psychologically. However there are more universal factors here. Now growing older is on the table, for everyone. It is not that aging was ignored before now, but rather that aging cannot be ignored, avoided, or denied now. Now the effects of so many decisions (marriage, divorce, children, work, house, etc.) made in earlier years are being felt. Concerns about the future surface in new ways. Financial and emotional well-being as well as physical health are primary concerns, and more than these concerns is the sense that one's usefulness and meaning in life may be changing or—one hopes not—coming to an end. This virtually unspoken sense that one's life is changing, one's role in life is changing, one's identity is changing is, like still water running deep, having a powerful influence on the course of one's aging. *The central focus and central meaning of life here: allow oneself to adapt successfully to an aging self, an aging body, an aging family, while undergoing aging itself and making room for new perspectives on one's focus and purpose in life. Grow one's identity to facilitate and embrace this expansion of self and survive aging.*

- Moving on through the life cycle, considering what persons in the later 70s and 80s are experiencing, as in Stories 36–40 (found in part six), we cannot help but realize how short life is. It was just yesterday that we were: children and thought of aging as happening to other people; or young adults and wanted to form careers and find mates; or somewhat older adults and wanted to make more money, make our families work, and not think too hard about ourselves growing older although wanting to be ready for its eventuality; or middle age adults grappling with the diverse pressures and pressing questions of being middle age; or later middle age adults feeling that growing older is going to happen, and not so far in the distant future as it once seemed; or persons on the border between later middle age and what follows, who are very aware that older ages are right around the corner; or older persons who are realizing that they are, for sure, what others and even they call old and or older people. *The central focus and central meaning of life here is: discover in one's aging a sense of self, a new and or renewed meaning, a deepening of the world view, spirit, sense of history, and significance of personal life story. Focus on the identity, the meaning of one's life, the daily and moment to moment value of one's life as well as the larger picture. Hold on to life, and its meaning.*

We can see the course of a lifetime in years. We can see the course of a lifetime in experiences that go with the various stages of our lives. We can see the course of a lifetime in terms of our perceptions of growing up and older and then old. Ideally, we are guided when we are young, and then guide ourselves as we grow older, to see aging in a positive light. It turns out that the younger we take on a positive view of our aging and of our future, the more positive our later aging will be. It is also true that optimism as we age, and when we are older, has a great influence on how we take our aging process. What this means is that a positive attitude is powerful.

We also know that finding meaning and usefulness in one's life can have a positive effect on the experience of aging. Meaning, and the usefulness it brings with it, can come to us in many different ways. Each of us must find the path to meaning in our lives that suits us. But we must find that meaning. For some, one or more passions such as painting, or nature, or a philosophy or spirituality of life, are great structures and give great meaning. Each of us must explore paths to making our lives mean something to us. Most likely, it will be more than one path that leads us to ourselves. All roads leading us to us are roads to meaning in life.

APPENDICES

Appendix A

Interview Questionnaire

BASIC BACKGROUND INFORMATION

1. What is your first and last name? (If you prefer only to give last initial this is OK. No real first or last names of interviewees will be used in the write-up or book.)

2. May we contact you if we would like a bit more information later, after this interview. We are not expecting to need this, but just in case? (If you prefer to say no, this is OK.) If so, please tell us how we can contact you later.

3. What is your age? (*Only if interviewee does not want to give age, then write an age range in here. Use age ranges found on tracking sheet.*)

4. What is your martial status: married, living with someone, living alone, and are you separated, divorced, and so on. (You can give more than one answer to this question.)

5. What is your living situation? (Do you live alone or with family, spouse, friends, people in a nursing home, or some other form of living situation.)

6. Are you presently employed, self-employed, retired, and so forth and can you say more about this?

7. Other background information offered by interviewee or asked by interviewer.

8. Interviewer: always be sure to write in the gender of the interviewee right here.

SPECIFIC ATTITUDES AND CONCERNS INFORMATION

1. Do you think about getting older? If so, what do you think?

2. What age ranges do getting older represent to you? (Is 30 old, is 40 old, is 50 old, and so on.)

3. If you have concerns about getting older, what are your greatest concerns?

4. Do you think there are positive aspects of getting older, and if so what are these?

5. Have you ever been divorced or have you ever experienced a breakup of a major relationship? If so, has this affected your thoughts about growing older? How?

6. Do you have children? If so how many? (Biological, step, adopted or other children—specify types of children you have if any.)

7. Do you think your children, step-children, and or future children (if you have not had children or all your children yet) will care for you when you are older? If so, how?

8. Have you ever cared for, or helped to take care of in any way, a parent or grandparent? If so, how? And if you did, how did this affect your views on aging?

9. Do you think about whether you will be alone as you get older. Is this an issue to you? (Perhaps you are not concerned, and this is also OK.)

10. Do you think about friends aging, or about how long they will be around, or whether they will be healthy and able to be in your life? If so what do you think about this matter?

11. Are there physical conditions and or diseases you are concerned about as you get older? Or as you look at getting older?

12. Are there things you want to do, or wish you had done differently to prepare for old age?

13. Do you think your children will help you at all as you get older? (Please respond whether or not you have children at this time, as these questions are for adults of all ages.)

14. Do you think about the economy now and the economy in the future? Do economic issues play a part in your thinking about getting older?

15. What is your view of Social Security and Medicare?

16. What does retirement mean to you? If you are not retired yet, do you look forward to it? What do you think it will be like for you? If you are already retired, how it is for you, what is it like for you?

General interviewee comments and concerns added to the above during this interview are to be placed here at the end, when you ask:

> Do you have other comments about getting older that you would like to share here? Are there things that we have not asked about that you think are important or interesting in some way?

Thank you very much for your participation in this study. You are helping increase the understanding of, and the dialog about, the aging process.

Again, the information you provide will not appear with your name. Much of the information you provide will be combined with the information provided by others to create a general story of attitudes about aging.

Appendix B

Problem-Solving Steps Explained

This appendix details some of the problem-solving steps discussed in chapter 23. Each step is listed below in bold type, and then that step is explained following the step itself. Note that being aware of one's mental problem-solving processes not only aids in problem solving itself, but also helps the mind stay active in selecting, directing, and integrating its functions—its attention, its concentration, its focus, its abilities to think, and to think about itself thinking. These are mental functions we want to have remain as active as they can be for us, at any and all ages. Keeping the mind alive and lively involves keeping the mind thinking and aware of its thinking processes.

Note your degree of familiarity with the problem

Have you been given a problem like this before? When? How often? Do you consider yourself used to/just getting used to/not very used to/not at all used to problems of this sort? What makes you think so? How do you know this?

Judge the type of problem

Is this a math problem or a science problem or an English problem or a communication problem or an interpersonal problem—or some other type of problem? How do you know what type of problem this is? What things about this problem tell you what kind of problem it is?

See this problem in your mind

Make a picture of this problem, or something that looks like a part of this problem, in your mind. If you do not have a picture, just make one up. There is no right or wrong here. Any picture or diagram in your mind is a good place to start. Or, if you can draw or sketch something about this problem on paper, do this first. Then, try to see this sketch in your mind. What would it look like if you saw it on television? Now try to diagram this problem—in steps or phases—perhaps using boxes or circles, and lines and arrows, in your diagram.

Try it on for size

Imagine that you can walk into this diagram, image, or picture you have imagined or drawn. Wander around in it. How does it look from the inside? Can you see it from different corners or sides of the inside? What about from various sides of the outside? What we are talking about is *physical imaging*. We can use our imaginations to act out problems we are trying to solve—to see them. We can use our memories and our imaginations to act out things that we've done before with our bodies—in order to *sense*—or visualize—the answers to our questions. When we do this, we are engaging in physical imaging.

Look closely at what your own thinking about how something works really depends on. Can you think about other ways that this something might work? Can you see other ways in your mind? Treat it as if it were an object. If it is an object, ask yourself to imagine how it works. What steers it? What happens if you don't turn it on? What happens if it is upside down?

I find that the ease with which I can do physical imaging depends on whether the thing is familiar, something that I have done before. I reach into my data bank and look for a picture of what ever it is I am thinking about. Let's say it is a bicycle—I am wondering how a bicycle really works. I reach into my mind and I find a memory of myself riding the bike. I ride the bike in my mind.

This same approach to seeing problems can be applied to problems that are less physical, for example, emotional and interpersonal problems. These can also be diagrammed or pictured in the mind. These can also be "walked around in" to be better understood.

Connect this problem to personal experience in the material world

What sorts of things that you have done (games you have played, work you have done with your hands such as building or cooking or drawing or playing with toys, etc.) help you think about problems like this one? Explain how these are connected in your mind. What activity does this problem remind you of?

Apply relevant principles

What do you know that you may need to know here? Are there specific rules or theories that you have been taught that are useful in thinking about this problem? If so, what are these? How do these apply?

Build on experience

Use everything you know to help you solve this problem. Search through your mind for things that might help you, that you would tend to overlook.

Break the problem into small steps

What do you do (think) first, second, third, and so on in solving this problem? What is the *sequence* of your thoughts? Think in small steps, specific pieces of the process.

Build on others' findings

If you are working on this problem with another person, or persons, ask each other each of the above questions. Then build on each other's way of solving this problem.

Build on your own findings after doing all the above

Once the above are underway or completed, then you have findings derived from all of the above efforts and other efforts in other arenas of your life. Build on these findings.

Use everything available to you to think this through

This means exactly this: Use everything and every bit of information available to you to think this through.

Keep your mind's executive control functions working and working hard throughout life. Be aware of their working and even encourage these to work consciously. Stay in touch with your mind, your thinking processes and how these are working.

Appendix C

Trauma, Aging, and Closure

Life has its upsets. Of these upsets, many are simple challenges calling to be resolved, and many are indeed resolved. However, there are also upsets that are more profound, and more difficult to resolve or move beyond in some way—or in any way. Some of these traumatic experiences are frequently experiences that shake us to the core, that disturb us for long periods of time following the experience itself, or for the rest of our lives. In recent times, we have heard a great deal regarding the post-traumatic stress (disorder or PTSD) that war veterans can experience. We now know that untreated PTSD can reveal itself many years after the traumatic event. It happens to be true that untreated PTSD can dig itself deeper and deeper into the psyche over time and become more difficult to overcome later.

Untreated anguish and trauma can pursue us into old age. Whether it be as a result of a war experience, or another severely upsetting and challenging event or even disaster, PTSD can linger and affect those it affects virtually every day for the rest of their lives. Too many victims of trauma experience a *deep lack of closure for years if not for the rest of their lives* (as the traumatic effect is frequently undetected, unseen for years or forever). Even when having been treated for the trauma, the treatment for this trauma may not really address the trauma itself. There can be a lingering sense of limbo in trauma, even of being stranded in a space that suggests there is closure—says that closure has taken place—but in which actual closure has never actually occurred.

The trauma and its effects, whether obvious or buried effects, can stay with us throughout our lives, even well into our older ages. In fact, far too many persons who have experienced trauma remain profoundly affected for life, with the effects reappearing or taking new forms sometimes years later. Furthermore, too often, the effects of trauma surface later in forms not identified with the original cause of the trauma. This makes the effects of the trauma all the more difficult for persons experiencing them to address.

A sense of free floating anxiety, fear, disconnection with natural emotional sequences, and other lingering emotional conditions, all can haunt and be triggered for no clear reason even years later. Hence, when one thinks particular memories are healed, and that one is years past the problem, the hand of this (untreated or incompletely treated) trauma reaches out and touches (or grabs) that person. Traces, almost indelible traces, of trauma and the emotional patterns that are developed as a result of trauma, can linger on. This makes us all the more susceptible to new traumatic experiences, or to new problem experiences that may feel traumatic in that they are compounding the hidden unresolved traumas buried deeply within but still quite active.

The sense of *being trapped in an unfinished experience*, stuck in a lack of closure state, troubles many persons who have experienced traumas. The lingering sense (even hidden sense) that a trauma is not complete, that the impact of the trauma lingers and is relived at the slightest reminder, must be addressed. However, once we move into old age, we are thought to be past the traumas we experienced earlier in life and not exposed to new present time traumas. (How can it be that persons in old age are viewed as suffering less simply because they are old?) All too often people enter old age carrying the baggage of unresolved and untreated trauma, and entirely vulnerable to being re-traumatized or newly traumatized by new events.

All too frequently, traumatized individuals bury their emotional turmoil and pain, growing numb to this on the surface but suffering inside all the same. Numbing while experiencing pain, suffering, and abuse is a coping mechanism, as is forgetting about the pain, suffering, and abuse. Forgetting can indeed be coping, however, this forgetting of the experience can be burying the experience deep in the subconscious mind. It lingers there, its conscious surface level sensations *blocked but not erased*. Forgetting serves as a barrier to remembering what has taken place, but not a barrier to the disturbance that what has happened leaves within.

The mind deals with traumatic experience in various ways, with the processes of numbing and forgetting being two. The mind is skilled at internal protective camouflage, and has the ability to convince, in this case, not the outside world but itself, that the camouflaged, distorted, reality it serves up to its consciousness, is real. Mental processes such as dissociation, in which the mind separates out normally connected mental processes from each other and from the rest of the mind, are a way of not seeing or processing these as *connected experiences*, as whole events. Painful memories, taken apart and served back up to ourselves fractured, are possibly less painful than when served up as a whole. This memory-fracturing process as a coping skill is then transferred to experience in the here and now, where the experience of present-time reality may also be dissociated from. Memories and current experiences become incompletely perceived and reacted to. As we age, the complex processes described here are further tied up in the emotional stages of aging, and in any accompanying distress and fear and loneliness that accompanies some people's aging processes.

There can be a deep buried need for a sense of closure when living with a history of pain, suffering and abuse, even after (and if) the visible, conscious, sense of closure has been reached. Sometimes the trauma of emotionally or physically violent experience lingers, hidden but present, and subtly affecting all aspects of one's existence for years, maybe decades and too often right on through the older age years. Pretending as if this is not the case does not make this not the case, rather it subjects some traumatized people to half-lives, never being entirely themselves. Given that we are indeed forever changed, on a very deep neurological level, by trauma, help to not only rebuild what can be salvaged of the self, but to construct a healed or new self, is essential—no matter what our ages may be.

Appendix D

Long-Term Intimate Partner Violence and Trauma Moving into Aging

A special note on long-term intimate and or spousal partner violence and abuse and related trauma. In long-term relationships where there are repeated incidents of emotional and physical violence over time, there can be trauma upon trauma upon trauma, continuously compounding the effects of each trauma. Trauma typically results in trauma-induced neurological change (discussed in appendix C) while burying conscious realization that one is actually traumatized.

Persons who are being hurt or abused may even cling to a dangerous pattern of pain, suffering and or abuse, not realizing that it may be the trauma itself perpetuating the pattern. The hunger for closure can leave the traumatized individual stuck in a pattern whose cycles may fool all involved and feel something like closure (while not really being closure) each time the cycle seems to end. As this individual moves into older age, this pattern can remain, and be relived externally or internally. Quite frequently, such troubled long-term trauma patterns move to deep levels where they work on the mind from inside. Aging with such untreated and unresolved patterns lurking deep inside can be painful, yet the source of the pain can be unacknowledged or even unrecognized for the rest of one's life.

Older couples who have long histories of emotional and physical abuse, can feel the effects of these patterns the rest of their lives, and even preserve these patterns in some way, oft while not realizing at all what is taking place. Their energy for actual physical abuse may dwindle, or it may continue in the same or a milder form. Their energy for actual emotional abuse is more readily continued and frequently does. Still, the older couples who are "used to" these painful patterns do not necessarily seek a change, or know anything different enough to seek a change.

For some, a change even for the better is more disturbing than staying locked in the same pattern. For example, when a member of a long-term marriage—in which the husband has abused the wife for the entire time they were together—loses her spouse, loses the spouse who abused her for decades, she may miss him no matter how abusive he was. (Note that the reverse of this, where the genders are the in the opposite abuser-abusee roles can result in much the same response.)

Appendix E

Emotional Abuse and Sadomasochism in Aging

Emotional abuse can occur in martial relationships, or among partners. It can also take place among family members or between hired caregivers and their clients. Emotional abuse is quite common and largely unrecognized, unseen. Its effects can be profound and far reaching, however all too often these effects are not traced back to their source when their source is emotional abuse.

Some emotional abuse is of a sadistic nature. Sadistic abuse is abuse that provides the abuser some pleasure while doing the abusing. This pleasure may be sexual, yes, as the common definition of physical sadomasochism suggests. However, here we are looking at emotional abuse in which the person doing the abusing feels some form of revenge or satisfaction or another pleasure while abusing. The sadistic emotional abuser may not realize that the drive to abuse is to experience some form of emotional reward while abusing.

Masochism is perhaps a strong word to use in this discussion. Masochism implies that the person being abused experiences some form of drive to be abused, that there is some form of reward in being abused. (I have discussed this matter in great detail in my book, *To Have and To Hurt: Seeing, Changing or Escaping Patterns of Abuse in Relationships*. I will not detail this in full here.) Where the person being abused has been involved in this pattern of abuse for many years, even decades, this pattern can become a given, an ongoing way of life for that person.

The possibility of any change away from a long-term pattern may be disturbing, and may be threatening enough that the person being abused prefers to stay in that role of abusee. This is not that there is a direct pleasure in being abused, but rather that that role of abusee may be all that the person being abused knows at this point. This role may appear to be safer than the alternative, which is to leave the relationship and be alone. In this sense, this drive to stay in the emotionally abusive relationship is similar to, or actually a form of, masochism.

Note: A further word about the sadomasochistic relationship. This is a challenging topic for a number of reasons. It is indeed generally assumed that sex has to be involved in this sort of relationship, with the person being described as the sadist taking sexual pleasure when causing someone else pain or suffering, and with the person being described as the masochist taking sexual pleasure in suffering or responding to the abuse someone, usually the sadist, is inflicting. Yet, for some purposes, these definitions of physical sadomasochism and masochism are close to accurate. However, there are many variations on what is called sadomasochism in daily life and daily relating, many of these not necessarily linked to sexual pleasure, and often not at all linked to sex in any way, and more often linked to emotional pain and pleasure.

Therefore, a special discussion of the sadomasochistic relationship is useful at this point in this discussion of emotional and physical abuse. A sadomasochistic relationship may or may not be one that includes the above-referred to sexual sadomasochism but it can and often does include elements of emotional sadism and or masochism. Emotional sadomasochism is a relationship pattern that is often hidden although existing right before our very eyes, with major components of the sadomasochistic process themselves invisible, nonphysical, emotional, and even non or pre-emotional (still buried deep enough in the subconsciousness that they are not registering consciously with any emotional or recognizable impact). In fact, these unseen elements play powerful roles, far more than we give them credit for. These hidden patterns are composed of intricate and often quite subtle energy exchange processes.

Appendix F

Elder Living Environment Checklist Suggestions with Sample Elder Living Environment Checklist

The following is a sample checklist, a form to be added to, personalized, by those who use it. This checklist is a template for conducting a personal review of the living environment one is living within, or placing a loved one in, or seeing a loved one living in. The goal here is to sensitize oneself to one's preferences regarding an older person's (or one's own) living environment. Too often, we are too close to a living situation to step back and see it in full.

Develop a checklist for reviewing an elder living environment, and continue to add to it over time. This checklist can have general categories, such as these listed below: Overall Quality of Physical Environment; Overall Quality of Social Environment; Overall Quality of Psychological Environment; Overall Quality of Spiritual Environment. Use these category names, or revise these, or add to these additional categories.

Within each category, you may want to add specific areas to look for, such has been done within these categories below. Also note that this checklist below has a built-in rating scheme, with 1 being the lowest score in an area and 5 being the highest. This can be used over time, to measure your own changing view of a living environment, or this can be used to measure changes that might be happening within that living environment, or this can be used to compare living environments.

SAMPLE ELDER LIVING ENVIRONMENT CHECKLIST

Note: Rate each area listed below, with 1 being the lowest rating, and 5 the highest rating. Circle your each of your ratings in each of these areas. Total all your rating scores (all numbers you have circled) at the bottom of this checklist.

If you are comparing more than one living environment, compare the totals on this checklist for each of these environments. If you are comparing a single living environment to itself over time, compare the total you give that environment on this checklist each time you reconsider that environment,

This is only a template. Amend or add to this list of questions as you find items to add, change, or remove.

Overall Quality of Physical Environment for the Individual	1	2	3	4	5
Environment is Accessible	1	2	3	4	5
Environment is Safe	1	2	3	4	5
Environment is Clean	1	2	3	4	5
Environment is Comfortable	1	2	3	4	5
Environment Provides Nutritional Meals	1	2	3	4	5
Environment is Suitable to Individual Needs	1	2	3	4	5
Environment is Attractive	1	2	3	4	5
Environment Offers Privacy	1	2	3	4	5
Other Characteristics of Physical Environment are Positive	1	2	3	4	5

Overall Quality of Social Environment for the Individual	1	2	3	4	5
Social Environment Exists	1	2	3	4	5
Social Environment Does Not Isolate People	1	2	3	4	5
Social Environment is Accessible	1	2	3	4	5
Social Environment is Safe	1	2	3	4	5
Social Environment is Interactive	1	2	3	4	5
Social Environment is to Individual Needs	1	2	3	4	5
Social Environment Does Allow for Privacy Where Needed	1	2	3	4	5
Other Characteristics of Social Environment are Positive	1	2	3	4	5

Overall Psychological Environment for the Individual	1	2	3	4	5
Psychological Environment	1	2	3	4	5
Psychological Environment Does Not Isolate People	1	2	3	4	5
Psychological Environment is Accessible	1	2	3	4	5
Psychological Environment is Safe	1	2	3	4	5
Psychological Environment is Interactive	1	2	3	4	5
Psychological Environment is Responsive To Individual Needs	1	2	3	4	5
Other Characteristics of Psychological are Positive	1	2	3	4	5

Overall Spiritual Environment for the Individual	1	2	3	4	5
Spiritual Environment Exists	1	2	3	4	5
Spiritual Environment is Responsive to Individual Needs	1	2	3	4	5
Spiritual Environment is Available to Persons Regardless Religious Orientation or Absence of a Spiritual Orientation	1	2	3	4	5
Spiritual Environment Does Not Isolate People	1	2	3	4	5
Spiritual Environment is Safe	1	2	3	4	5
Other Characteristics of Spiritual Environment are Positive	1	2	3	4	5

The following is an additional checklist section for rating quality of the elder living environment for those who visit that individual (e.g., family and friends).

Overall Quality of the Elder's Living Environment for Friends and Family	1	2	3	4	5
Environment is Accessible for Visiting	1	2	3	4	5
Environment is Welcoming to Visitors	1	2	3	4	5
Environment Accommodates Visitors	1	2	3	4	5
Environment Visiting Hours are Acceptable	1	2	3	4	5
Other Characteristics of Quality of Environment for Visitors are Positive	1	2	3	4	5

Appendix G

Resources

The following list of online resources is but a sample of the many organizational and governmental sources of information and research relating to issues of aging and the life cycle. Some of these organizations are governmental and others are private.

PRIVATE ORGANIZATIONS

American Association of Retired Persons (AARP)

The AARP is a membership organization leading advocacy for the elder population, positive social change, and providing other resources. **www. aarp.org**

American Society on Aging (ASA)

The ASA is the largest organization of multidisciplinary professionals in the field of aging. Our resources, publications, and educational opportunities are geared to enhance the knowledge and skills of people working with older adults and their families. **www.asaging.org**

International Longevity Center (ILC)

Founded in 1990 by world-renowned gerontologist and Pulitzer Prize winner, Robert N. Butler, MD, the ILC is the first nonprofit, nonpartisan, international research, policy, and education organization formed to educate individuals on how to live longer and better, and advise society on how to maximize the benefits of today's age boom. **http://www.ilcusa.org/**

National Council on the Aging (NCOA)

The National Council on Aging is a nonprofit service and advocacy organization headquartered in Washington, DC, whose mission is to improve the lives of older Americans. The NCOA is a national voice for older adults—especially those who are vulnerable and disadvantaged—and the community organizations that serve them. The NCOA brings together nonprofit organizations, businesses, and government to develop creative solutions that improve the lives of all older adults. The NCOA works with thousands of organizations across the country to help seniors live independently, find jobs and benefits, improve their health, live independently and remain active in their communities: **www.ncoa.org**

ADDITIONAL RESOURCES

Benefits Checkup (NCOA)

A service of the National Council on Aging. **http://www.benefits checkup.org/**

Medicare NewsWatch.com

Dedicated to helping seniors make decisions about Medicare Advantage plans. **www.MedicareNewsWatch.com**

GOVERNMENTAL RESOURCES

American Federation for Aging Research (AFAR)

This organization has helped scientists begin and further careers in aging research and geriatric medicine. **http://www.afar.org/**

Alzheimer's Association

A national network of chapters, this is the largest national voluntary health organization dedicated to advancing Alzheimer's research and helping those affected by the disease. Having awarded $136 million in research grants, the association ranks as the top private funder of research into the causes, treatments, and prevention of Alzheimer's Disease. This association also provides education and support for people diagnosed with the condition, their families, and caregivers. **http://www.alz.org/ index.asp**

Eldercare Locator

Eldercare Locator is a public service of the U.S. Administration on Aging. The Eldercare Locator is your first step for finding local agencies, in every U.S. community, which can help older persons and their families access home and community-based services like transportation, meals, home care, and caregiver support services. **www.eldercare.gov**

National Eye Institute (NEI)

The NEI conducts and supports research that helps prevent and treat eye diseases and other disorders of vision. This research leads to sight-saving treatments, reduces visual impairment and blindness, and improves the quality of life for people of all ages. The NEI-supported research has advanced our knowledge of how the eye functions in health and disease. **http://www.nei.nih.gov/**

National Heart, Lung, and Blood Institute (NHLBI)

The NHLBI provides leadership for a national program in diseases of the heart, blood vessels, lung, and blood; blood resources; and sleep disorders. Since October 1997, the NHLBI has also had administrative responsibility for the NIH Woman's Health Initiative. The institute plans, conducts, fosters, and supports an integrated and coordinated program of basic research, clinical investigations and trials, observational studies, and demonstration and education projects. **http://www.nhlbi.nih.gov/ index.htm**

National Human Genome Research Institute (NHGRI)

The NHGRI supports the NIH component of the Human Genome Project, a worldwide research effort designed to analyze the structure of human DNA and determine the location of the estimated 30,000 to 40,000 human genes. The NHGRI Intramural Research Program develops and implements technology for understanding, diagnosing, and treating genetic diseases. **http://www.genome.gov/**

National Institute on Aging (NIA)

The NIA leads a national program of research on the biomedical, social, and behavioral aspects of the aging process; the prevention of age-related diseases and disabilities; and the promotion of a better quality of life for all older Americans. **http://www.nia.nih.gov/**

National Institute on Alcohol Abuse and Alcoholism (NIAAA)

The NIAAA conducts research focused on improving the treatment and prevention of alcoholism and alcohol-related problems to reduce the enormous health, social, and economic consequences of this disease. **http://www.niaaa.nih.gov/**

National Institute of Allergy and Infectious Diseases (NIAID)

The NIAID research strives to understand, treat, and ultimately prevent the myriad infectious, immunologic, and allergic diseases that threaten millions of human lives. **http://www3.niaid.nih.gov/**

National Institute of Arthritis and Musculoskeletal and Skin Diseases (NIAMS)

The NIAMS supports research into the causes, treatment, and prevention of arthritis and musculoskeletal and skin diseases, the training of basic and clinical scientists to carry out this research, and the dissemination of information on research progress in these diseases. **http://www. niams.nih.gov/**

National Institute of Biomedical Imaging and Bioengineering (NIBIB)

The NIBIB improves health by promoting fundamental discoveries, design and development, and translation and assessment of technological capabilities in biomedical imaging and bioengineering, enabled by relevant areas of information science, physics, chemistry, mathematics, materials science, and computer sciences. **http://www.nibib.nih.gov/**

National Institute on Deafness and Other Communication Disorders (NIDCD)

The NIDCD conducts and supports biomedical research and research training on normal mechanisms as well as diseases and disorders of hearing, balance, smell, taste, voice, speech, and language that affect 46 million Americans. **http://www.nidcd.nih.gov/**

National Institute of Dental and Craniofacial Research (NIDCR)

The NIDCR provides leadership for a national research program designed to understand, treat, and ultimately prevent the infectious and inherited craniofacial-oral-dental diseases and disorders that compromise millions of human lives. **http://www.nidcr.nih.gov/**

National Institute of Diabetes and Digestive and Kidney Diseases (NIDDK)

The NIDDK conducts and supports basic and applied research and provides leadership for a national program in diabetes, endocrinology, and metabolic diseases; digestive diseases and nutrition; and kidney, urologic, and hematologic diseases. Several of these diseases are among the leading causes of disability and death; all seriously affect the quality of life of those who have them. **http://www2.niddk.nih.gov/**

National Institute on Drug Abuse (NIDA)

The NIDA leads the nation in bringing the power of science to bear on drug abuse and addiction through support and conduct of research across a broad range of disciplines and rapid and effective dissemination of results of that research to improve drug abuse and addiction prevention, treatment, and policy. **http://www.nida.nih.gov/**

National Institute of Environmental Health Sciences (NIEHS)

The NIEHS reduces the burden of human illness and dysfunction from environmental causes by defining how environmental exposures, genetic susceptibility, and age interact to affect an individual's health. **http://www.niehs.nih.gov/**

National Institute of General Medical Sciences (NIGMS)

The NIGMS supports basic biomedical research that is not targeted to specific diseases. The institute funds studies on genes, proteins, and cells, as well as on fundamental processes like communication within and between cells, how our bodies use energy, and how we respond to medicines. The results of this research increase our understanding of life and lay the foundation for advances in disease diagnosis, treatment, and prevention. The NIGMS also supports research training programs that produce the next generation of biomedical scientists, and it has special programs to encourage underrepresented minorities to pursue biomedical research careers. **http://www.nigms.nih.gov/**

National Institute of Mental Health (NIMH)

The NIMH provides national leadership dedicated to understanding, treating, and preventing mental illnesses through basic research on the brain and behavior, and through clinical, epidemiological, and services research. **http://www.nimh.nih.gov/index.shtml**

Warren Grant Magnuson Clinical Center (CC)

The CC is the clinical research facility of the National Institutes of Health. As a national resource, it provides the patient care, services, and environment needed to initiate and support the highest quality conduct of and training in clinical research. **http://www.cc.nih.gov/**

Appendix H

Religious and Spiritual Perspectives on Aging and Resources

ANNOTATED BIBLIOGRAPHY ON RELIGION, SPIRITUALITY, AND AGING

http://tech.union-psce.edu/aging and www.gracefulaging.org

Complied by Henry Simmons, Union Theological Seminary professor, an extensive online resource on aging, religion, and spirituality addressing spiritual, religious, ethical, and other topics.

Center for Aging and Spirituality

www.spirituality4aging.org

The Center for Aging and Spirituality, based in Cupertino, California, began as a monthly reading group for Lutheran chaplains, and now offers workshops on aging for older adults, family members and professionals.

Faith-Based Programs in Aging

www.aoa.gov/prof/notes/notes_faithbased_services.asp

This Web site lists the guide, compiled by the Administration on Aging to "national and local, denominational and interdenominational" faith-based services for older adults.

Forum on Religion, Spirituality, and Aging

www.asaging.org/forsa

> The FORSA offers resources and notes regarding networking in the fields of aging and spirituality.

Gerotranscendence

www.soc.uu.se/research/gerontology/gerotrans.html

> Here, author of *Gerotranscendence: A Developmental Theory of Positive Aging*, Lars Tornstam, addresses and related issues to his theory, gerotranscendence: "a shift in meta-perspective, from a materialistic and rational view of the world to a more cosmic and transcendent one, normally accompanied by an increase in life satisfaction."

Listmania: Spirituality and Aging

www.amazon.com

> Pastor Carla Libby Gentry has compiled this list on spirituality and aging found on Amazon.com that recommends books on spirituality and aging.

Overview of Religion, Spirituality, and Aging?

http://cas.umkc.edu/casww/sa/Spirituality.htm

> University of Missouri, Kansas City, Lois Fitzpatrick provides an overview on spirituality as it pertains to aging, and addresses strategies to bring spirituality into elders' lives.

Sacred Seasons

www.sacredseasons.org

> The Center for Aging and Judaism at the Reconstructionist Rabbinical College, Hiddur, offers this "Sacred Seasons" kit to enhance holidays and Shabbat services for elders in nursing homes and other settings where they might not be able to participate in Jewish life.

Spiritual Gerontology

www.senioradultministry.com/category.aspx?categoryID = 29

> The Johnson Institute for Maturing Adult Faith Formation and Spiritual Gerontology offers this Web site to share lessons of the Reverend Richard Johnson regarding Christian perspectives in aging.

Bibliography

Abel, E. 1986. "Adult Daughters and Care for the Elderly." *Feminist Studies* 12:279–497.

Abele, N., S. Cooley, I. M. Deitch, M. S. Harper, G. Hinrichsen, M. A. Lopez, and V. A. Molinari. 1997. *What Practitioners Should Know About Working With Older Adults*. Washington, DC: American Psychological Association.

Aday, R. H. 1988. *Crime and the Elderly: An Annotated Bibliography*. New York: Greenwood Press.

Ahlburg, D. A., and C. J. De Vita. 1992. "New Realities of the American Family." *Population Bulletin* 47 (2, August).

Aldous, J. 1995. "New Views on Grandparents in Intergenerational Context." *Journal of Family Issues* 16 (1, January): 104–22.

Allen, J., and A. Pifer, eds. 1993. *Women on the Front Lines: Meeting the Challenge of an Aging America*. Washington, DC: Urban Institute Press.

Alon-Shenker, P. 2007. Revisiting the Legal Doctrine of Age Discrimination in the Employment Setting. Paper presented at the annual meeting of The Law and Society Association, TBA, Berlin, Germany, July 24. http://www.allacademic.com/meta/p175644_index.html

American Association of Retired Persons (AARP). 1991a. *The Contingent Workforce: Implications for Midlife and Older Women. Fact Sheet. Women's Initiative*. Washington, DC: Author.

American Geriatrics Society and American Association for Geriatric Psychiatry. 2003. "Consensus Statement on Improving the Quality of Mental Health Care in US Nursing Homes: Management of Depression and Behavioral Symptoms Associated with Dementia." *Journal of the American Geriatrics Society* 51 (9): 1287–98.

American Geriatrics Society and American Association for Geriatric Psychiatry. 2003. "The American Geriatrics Society and American Association for Geriatric Psychiatry Recommendations for Policies in Support of Quality Mental Health Care in US Nursing Homes." *Journal of the American Geriatrics Society* 51 (9): 1299–1304.

American Society on Aging. 1997. *The Blues, Not a Normal Part of Aging: Coordinator's Manual.* Program kit. San Francisco: Author.

Andersson, L. 2002. *Cultural Gerontology.* Westport, CT: Praeger Publications.

Atkinson, D. R., and G. Hackett, eds. 1998. *Counseling Diverse Populations.* 2nd ed. New York: McGraw-Hill.

Auerbach, A. J. 2004. "Intergenerational Transfers and Savings Behavior: Comment Perspectives on the Economics of Aging." In NBER Conference Report Series, ed. D. A. Wise, 201–3. Chicago and London: University of Chicago Press.

Auerbach, A. J., and L. J. Kotlikoff. 2004. An Examination of Empirical Tests of Social Security and Saving. Working Paper No. 730, University of California–Berkeley, Department of Economics and Boston University, Department of Economics NBER.

Auerbach, A. J., and L. J. Kotlikoff. 2004. Life Insurance Inadequacy—Evidence From a Sample of Older Widows. Working Paper No. 3765, University of California–Berkeley, Department of Economics and Boston University, Department of Economics NBER.

Auerbach, A. J., and L. J. Kotlikoff. 2004. Life Insurance of the Elderly: Adequacy and Determinants. Working Paper No. 1737, University of California–Berkeley, Department of Economics and Boston University, Department of Economics NBER.

Auerbach, A. J., and L. J. Kotlikoff. 2004. The Efficiency Gains from Social Security Benefit—Tax Linkage. Working Paper No. 1645, University of California–Berkeley, Department of Economics and Boston University, Department of Economics NBER.

Baker, D. W., J. Gazmarmarian, J. Sudano, and M. Patterson. 2000. "The Association Between Age and Health Literacy Among Elderly Persons." *Journal of Gerontology* 55B (6): 368–74.

Ballard, C., J. O'Brien I. James, P. Mynt, M. Lana, D. Potkins, K. Reichelt, L. Lee, A. Swann, and J. Fossey. 2001. "Quality of Life for People with Dementia Living in Residential and Nursing Home Care: The Impact of Dependency, Behaviour and Psychotropic Drugs." *International Psychogeriatrics* 13 (1): 93–106.

Baltes, P. B., and P. Graf. 1996. "Psychological Aspects of Aging: Facts and Frontiers." In *The Lifespan Development of Individuals: Behavioral, Neurobiological, and Psychosocial Perspectives,* ed. D. Magnusson. Cambridge, England: Cambridge University Press.

Barber, C. J. 1984. "Marriage, Divorce or Remarriage: A Review of the Relevant Religious Literature, 1973–1983." *Journal of Psychology and Theology* 12 (Fall): 170–77.

Beresford, T., and E. Gomberg. 1995. *Alcohol and Aging*. New York: Oxford University Press.

Bilbo, S. D., and J. M. Schwarz. 2009. "Early-Life Programming of Later-Life Brain and Behavior: A Critical Role for the Immune System. *Frontiers in Behavioral Neuroscience* 3 (14): doi:10.3389/neuro.08.014.2009.

Birren, J. E., and K. W. Schaie, eds. 1996. *Handbook of the Psychology of Aging*. 4th ed. San Diego, CA: Academic Press.

Birren, J. E., R. B. Sloane, and G. D. Cohen, eds. 1992. *Handbook of Mental Health and Aging*. San Diego, CA: Academic Press.

Blazer, D. 1990. *Emotional Problems in Later Life*. New York: Springer Publishing Company.

Brehony, K. 1996. *Awakening At Midlife*. New York: Riverhead Books.

Bridges, W. 1980. *Transitions: Making Sense of Life's Changes*. Reading, MA: Addison-Wesley Publishing Company.

Browne-Miller, A. 2010. *Rewiring Yourself to Break Addictions and Habits*. Westport, CT: Praeger Publications.

Browne-Miller, A. 2008. *To Have and To Hurt*. Westport, CT: Praeger Publications.

Bunce, D., R. Handley, S. O. Gaines, Jr. 2008. "Depression, Anxiety, and Within-Person Variability in Adults Aged 18 to 85 Years." *Psychology and Aging* 23 (4): 848–58.

Burton, L. 1993. *Families and Aging*. Amityville, NY: Baywood.

Cadena, C. 2007. Women and Aging: Adult Children Caring for Aging Parents: Factors to Consider. *AC Associated Content*, March 16, 2007. http://www.associatedcontent.com/article/155813/women_and_aging_adult_children_caring.html?cat=12 (accessed May 10, 2009).

Callahan, J. C., ed. 1993. *Menopause: A Midlife Passage*. Bloomington, IN: Indiana University Press.

Center for Substance Abuse Prevention. 1994–1998. *Technical Assistance Bulletins: Guides for Planning and Developing Your ATOD Prevention Materials*. Rockville, MD: Division of Public Education and Dissemination.

Centers for Disease Control and Prevention. 1999. "Surveillance for Selected Public Health Indicators Affecting Older Adults—United States." *Morbidity and Mortality Weekly Report*, 48(SS-8). Washington, DC: Government Printing Office.

Cherry, K. E., N. Jamhour, and P. B. Mincey. 2004. "Aged by Culture" (review). *Biography* 27 (3): 631–34.

Cohen-Mansfield, J. 1986. "Agitated Behaviors in the Elderly, II: Preliminary Results in the Cognitively Deteriorated." *Journal of the American Geriatrics Society* 34:722–27.

Cohen Praver, F. 2004. *Crossroads at Midlife*. Westport, CT: Praeger Publications.

Cohler, B., and R. Galatzer-Levy. 1990. "The Selfobjects of the Second Half of Life: An Introduction." In *Progress in Self Psychology*, ed. A. Goldberg, Vol. 6, 93–109. New York: Guilford Press.

Coleman, P. G. 1999. "Self and Identity in Advanced Old Age: Validation of Theory Through Longitudinal Case Analysis." *Journal of Personality* 67 (5): 819–49.

Colleran, C., and D. Jay. 2002. *Aging and Addiction: Helping Older Adults Overcome Alcohol or Medication Dependence*. Deerfield Beach, FL: Hazelden Publishing.

Committee on Population (CPOP) and Behavioral and Social Sciences and Education (DBASSE). 2006. *Aging in Sub-Saharan Africa: Recommendations for Furthering Research*. Washington, DC: National Academies Press.

Conway, J. 1997. *Men in Mid-Life Crisis*. Colorado Springs, CO: Chariot Victor Publishing.

Coyle, J. M., ed. 2001. *Handbook on Women and Aging*. Westport, CT: Praeger Publications.

deAngelis, A. 2008. *Endings are Beginnings*. Flagstaff, AZ: LT Publications.

Deats, S. M., and L. T. Lenker. 1999. *Aging and Identity: A Humanities Perspective*. Westport, CT: Praeger Publications

Ebersole, P., and P. Hess. 1998. *Towards Healthy Aging: Human Needs and Nursing Response*. 5th ed. St. Louis, MO: Mosby-Year Book, Inc.

Edelman, P. 2001. "Improving Family Caregiver-Resident Interaction in a Long-Term Care Facility." *Northwestern Alzheimer's Disease Center News* 15 (Winter): 6.

Edelman, P., M. Guihan, D. Munroe, S. Miskevics, K. Clark, and J. M. Erdman. 2005. "Study Shows Assisted Living Continues to Hit the Mark on Satisfaction." *Assisted Living Executive* 12 (3): 37–38.

Ekerdt, D. J., ed. 2002. *Encyclopedia of Aging*, Vols. 1–4. New York: Macmillan Reference USA.

Eldridge, A. 1997. "Walking into the Eye of the Storm: Encountering "Repressed Memories" in the Therapeutic Context." In *Progress in Self Psychology*, ed. A. Goldberg, Vol. 13, 69–84. Hillsdale, NJ: The Analytic Press.

Elson, M. 1986. "Self Psychology and the Aging Process." In *Self Psychology in Clinical Social Work*. New York: W.W. Norton & Company.

Ferraro, K., and M. Farmer. 1996. "Double Jeopardy, Aging as Leveler, or Persistent Health Inequality? A Longitudinal Analysis of White and Black Americans." *Journal of Gerontology* 51B:S319–28.

Fodor, I. G., and V. Franks 1990. "Women in Midlife and Beyond: The New Prime of Life?" *Psychology of Women Quarterly* 14:445–49.

Forstmeier, S., and A. Maercker. 2008. "Motivational Reserve: Lifetime Motivational Abilities Contribute to Cognitive and Emotional Health in Old Age." *Psychology and Aging* 23 (4): 886–99.

Freidson, E. 1988. "The Lay Construction of Illness." In *Profession of Medicine*, 278–301. Chicago, IL: The University of Chicago Press.

Freidson, E. 1988. "The Professional Construction of Illness." In *Profession of Medicine* 244–77. Chicago, IL: The University of Chicago Press.

Friend, R. A. 1991. "Older Lesbian and Gay People: A Theory of Successful Aging. *Journal of Homosexuality* 20 (3–4): 99–118.

Fusco Johnson, T. 1991. *Elder Mistreatment*. Westport, CT: Praeger Publications.

Gatz, M., ed. 1995. *Emerging Issues in Mental Health and Aging*. Washington, DC: American Psychological Association.

Gaugler, J. E., K. A. Anderson, S. H. Zarit, and L. I. Pearlin. 2004. "Family Involvement in Nursing Homes: Effects on Stress and Wellbeing." *Aging and Mental Health* 8 (1): 65–75.

Gergen, M. M. 1990. "Finished at 40: Women's Development Within the Patriarchy." *Psychology of Women Quarterly* 14:471–93.

Glasgow, R. E. 1998. State of the Science and Practice: Exercise and Nutrition. Paper commissioned by the National Institute on Aging for an invited conference on "How Managed Care Can Help Older Persons Live Well with Chronic Conditions," Washington, DC.

Global Ageing Network Blog. Important Information on Global Ageing. http://iahsa.wordpress.com/tag/community-care/ (accessed December 2009).

Goldscheider, F. K., A. E. Biddlecom, and J. McNally 1994. Dependency, Privacy, and Power in Intergenerational Households: Changes in the Living Arrangements of the Elderly in the U.S., 1940–1990. Paper presented at the annual meeting of the American Sociological Association, Los Angeles, CA.

Grambs, J. D. 1989. *Women over Forty: Visions and Realities*. New York: Springer Publishing Company.

Greathouse, J. 2000. Learning New Tricks: Changing Behaviors to Improve Health. Presentation at the American Society on Aging Summer Series on Aging, July 13, San Francisco, CA.

Gurnack, A., ed., 1997. *Older Adults' Misuse of Alcohol, Medicines, and Other Drugs: Research and Practice Issues*. New York: Springer Publishing Company.

Guttman, D. 2008. *Finding Meaning In Life, At Midlife And Beyond: Wisdom and Spirit from Logotherapy*. Westport, CT: Praeger Publications.

Harvard School of Public Health—Metlife Foundation Initiative on Retirement and Civic Engagement. 2004. Reinventing Aging: Babyboomers and Civic Engagement. Cambridge, MA: Center for Health Communication, Harvard School of Public Health. http://www.hsph.harvard.edu/chc/rein ventingaging/Report.pdf

Hayslip, B., Jr., H. L. Servaty, and A. S. Ward. 1995. *Psychology of Aging: An Annotated Bibliography*. Westport, CT: Greenwood.

Hayutin, A. 2007. Global Aging, The New New Thing: The Big Picture of Population Change. Stanford Center on Longevity, Palo Alto, CA. http://lon gevity1.stanford.edu/files/GlobalAgingTheNewNewThing.pdf (accessed September 1, 2009).

Henretta, J. C., E. Y. Grundy, and S. Harris. 2001. "Socioeconomic Differences in Having Living Parents and Children: A U.S.-British Comparison of Middle-Aged Women. *Journal of Marriage and Family* 63:852–67.

Herbert, W. 2007. The Aging of Loneliness. http://www.psychologicalscience. org/onlyhuman/2007/08/aging-of-loneliness.cfm (accessed July 10, 2009).

Hertzberg, A., and S. L. Ekman. 2003. "We, Not Them and Us?": Views on the Relationships Between Staff and Relatives of Older People Permanently Living in Nursing Homes." *Journal of Advanced Nursing* 31 (3): 614–22.

Herzog, A. R., R. L. Kahn, J. N. Morgan, J. S. Jackson, and T. C. Antonucci. 1989. "Age Differences in Productive Activities." *Journal of Gerontology* 44:S129–38.

Hitti, M. 2008. 10 Health Aging Tips from Centenarians. *WebMD. Medicine.Net* http://www.medicinenet.com/script/main/art.asp?articlekey=91430 (accessed July 30, 2009).

Hollinger-Smith, L. M. 2000. "Developmental Aspects Across the Lifespan: The Elderly." In *Psychiatric-Mental Health Nursing,* eds. K. Fortinash and P. Holoday-Worret, 208–30. St. Louis. MO: Mosby.

Hollinger-Smith, L. M. 2001. *Building and Sustaining Community Partnerships: Models for Nursing Practice. The Nursing Profession: Tomorrow and Beyond,* ed. N. Chaska, 547–59. Thousand Oaks, CA: Sage Publications, Inc.

Hollinger-Smith, L. M. 2001. "Make a Job in Long-Term Care Your Short-Term Goal." *Nursing Spectrum* 14 (7IL):6–7.

Hollinger-Smith, L. M. 2003. Growth and Development Across the Life Span. Psychiatric Mental Health Nursing, ed. K. M. Fortinash and P. A. Holoday Worret, 138–70. 3rd ed. St. Louis, MO: Mosby.

Hollinger-Smith, L. M. 2003. "How to Care for an Aging Nation: Start with Educating the Educators." *Journal of Gerontological Nursing* 29 (3): 23–27.

Hollinger-Smith, L. M., D. Lindeman, M. S. Leary, and A. Ortigara. 2002. "Building the Foundation for Quality Improvement: LEAP for a Quality Long Term Care Workforce." *Senior Housing & Care Journal* 10 (1): 32–43.

Hollinger-Smith, L. M., and A. Ortigara. 2004. "Changing Culture: Creating a Long-Term Impact for a Quality Long-Term Care Workforce." *Alzheimer's Care Quarterly* 5 (1): 60–70.

Hollinger-Smith, L. M., A. Ortigara, and D. Lindeman. 2001. "Developing a Comprehensive Long-Term Care Workforce Initiative." *Alzheimer's Care Quarterly* 2 (3): 33–40.

Hurd, M. 1997. *Effective Therapy.* New York: Dunhill.

Ilan, T. 1996. "Notes and Observations on a Newly Published Divorced Bill from the Judaean Desert." *Harvard Theological Review* 89 (April): 195–202.

Keenan, T. A. 2000. Delivering Wellness to Boomers: What Do They Really Want? Presentation at the American Society on Aging 46th Annual Meeting, March 24–28, San Diego, CA.

Keller, C., and J. Fleury. 2000. *Health Promotion for the Elderly.* Thousand Oaks, CA: Sage Publications.

Kenyon, G. 2000. *Ordinary Wisdom.* Westport, CT: Praeger Publications.

Kern, M. L., and H. S. Friedman. 2008. "Early Educational Milestones as Predictors of Lifelong Academic Achievement, Midlife Adjustment, and Longevity." *Journal of Applied Developmental Psychology* 30 (4): 419–30.

Kimmel, D. C., and H. R. Moody. 1990. "Ethical Issues in Gerontological Research and Services." In *Handbook of the Psychology of Aging*, 490–502. New York: Academic Press.

Kramarow, E. 1995. "Living Alone Among the Elderly in the United States: Historical Perspectives on Household Change." *Demography* 32:335–52.

Krieger, D. T., and J. C. Hughes. 1980. *Neuroendocrinology: The Interrelationships of the Body's Two Major Integrative Systems in Normal Physiology and in Clinical Disease*. Sunderland, MA: Sinauer Associates, Incorporated.

Kuhn, D. 2004. "Caring from Afar: Meeting the Challenges of Long Distance Caregiving." *Chicago Caregiver* November–December: 16–19.

Kuhn, D., R. Kasayka, and C. Lechner. 2002. "Behavioral Observations and Quality of Life Among Residents with Dementia in Ten Assisted Living Facilities." *The American Journal of Alzheimer's Disease and Other Dementias* 17 (5): 291–98.

Kuhn, D., and K. Shannon. 2004. "National Program Gives Caregivers Powerful Tools." *Aging Today* 25 (5): 13–15.

Lamb, K., R. Engel, and L. M. Hollinger-Smith. 2005. "Exercise and Fall Reduction in Assisted Living." *Assisted Living Consult* September/October: 13–22.

Lamb, S. E. 2009. *Aging and the Indian Diaspora: Cosmopolitan Families in India and Abroad*. Bloomington, IN: Indiana University Press.

Lang, F., and K. Fingerman, eds. 2004. *Growing Together: Personal Relationships Across the Lifespan*. New York: Cambridge University Press.

Langley, L. K., P. D. Rokke, A. C. Stark, A. L. Saville, J. L. Allen, A. G. Bagne. 2008. "The Emotional Blink: Adult Age Differences in Visual Attention to Emotional Information." *Psychology and Aging* 23 (4): 873–85.

Lavin, M., ed. 2008. *The Oldest We Have Ever Been: Seven True Stories of Midlife Transitions*. Tucson, AZ: University of Arizona Press.

Lawton, M., J. Teresi, L. Grant, D. Lindeman, and R. Montgomery. 2002. "The Therapeutic Environment Screening Survey for Nursing Homes (TESS-NH): An Observation Instrument for Assessing the Physical Environment of Institutional Settings for Persons with Dementia." *Journal of Gerontology: Social Sciences* 57B (2): S69–S78.

Lazarus, L. 1988. "Self Psychology: Its Application to Brief Psychotherapy with the Elderly." *Journal of Geriatric Psychiatry* 21:109–25.

Levy, B. R., M. D. Slade, S. R. Kunkel, S. V. Kasl. 2002. "Longevity Increased by Positive Self-Perceptions of Aging." *Journal of Personality and Social Psychology* 83 (2): 261–70.

Lillard, L. 1996. Socioeconomic Differentials in the Returns to Social Security. Working Paper Series 96–05, Rand L&P.

Litwin, H. 1995. *Uprooted in Old Age*. Westport, CT: Praeger Publications.

Lo, Chi. 2006. China's Aging Problem: Limited Options, Ominous Risk. *Farlex: The Free Library*, September 26. http://www.thefreelibrary.com/China's+ aging+problem:+limited+options,+ominous+risk-a0154866721 (accessed July 1, 2009).

Luken, P. C. 1987. "Social Identity in Later Life: A Situational Approach to Understanding Old Age Stigma." *International Journal of Aging and Human Development* 25 (3): 177–93.

Lynch, V. 1988. "Discussion: Self Psychology—Its Application to Brief Psychotherapy with the Elderly." *Journal of Geriatric Psychiatry* 21:127–32.

Martin, L., and K. Kinsella. 1994. "Research on the Demography of Aging in Developing Countries." In *Demography of Aging*, eds. L. Martin and S. Preston, 356–403. Washington, DC: National Academy Press.

Mcnally, M. D. 2009. *Honoring Elders: Aging, Authority, and Ojibwe Religion (Religion and American Culture)*. New York: Columbia University Press.

Murguia, E., E. Schultz, T. M. Schultz, K. S. Markides, P. Janson. 1984. *Ethnicity and Aging: A Bibliography;* Part of the Humanities and Education Series #8. San Antonio, TX: Trinity University.

Muslin, H., and S. Clarke. 1988. "The Transference of the Therapist of the Elderly." *Journal of the American Academy of Psychoanalysis* 16:295–315.

Mutran, E., and P. J. Burke. 1979. "Personalism as a Component of Old Age Identity." *Research on Aging* 1 (1): 37–63.

National Bureau of Economic Research. 2007. Economics of Aging Program. Page 1. http://www.nber.org/aging.html (accessed October 3, 2009).

O'Brien Cousins, S. 1995. "The Life Situation Determinants of Exercise in Women Over the Age of 70." In *Physical Activity, Aging and Sports: Toward Healthy Aging: International Perspectives*, eds. S. Harris, W. S. Harris, and E. Heikkinen. Albany: Center for the Study on Aging.

O'Brien Cousins, S. 2000. " 'My Heart Couldn't Take It': Older Women's Beliefs About Exercise Benefits and Risks." *Journal of Gerontology: Psychological Sciences* 55B (5): 283–94.

Osgood, N. J., comp., H. E. Wood, ed., comp., I. A. Parham, ed. 1995. *Alcoholism and Aging: An Annotated Bibliography and Review*. Westport, CT: Greenwood Publishing Group.

Perry, S., and G. Heidrich. 1982. "Management of Pain during Debridement: A Survey of US Burn Units." *Pain* 12:267.

Pipher, M. 2001. "Society Fears the Aging Process." In *Opposing Viewpoints: Aging Population*, ed. L. K. Egendorf. San Diego, CA: Greenhaven Press. http://www.enotes.com/aging-population-article/40118 (accessed October 8, 2009).

Porter, J., H. Jick. 1980. "Addiction Rare in Patients Treated with Narcotics." *New England Journal of Medicine* 302 (2): 123

Preston, S. 1984. "Children and the Elderly: Divergent Paths for America's Dependents." *Demography* 21 (4):435–57.

Prochaska, J. O., J. C. Norcross, and C. C. DiClemente. 1994. *Changing for Good.* New York: Avon Books, Inc.

Ready, R. E., J. O. Carvalho, and M. I. Weinberger. 2008. "Emotional Complexity in Younger, Midlife, and Older Adults. *Psychology and Aging* 23 (4): 928–33.

Rubenstein, L. Z. 1996. "Update on Preventative Medicine for Older People." *Generations* 20 (4): 47–53.

Ruggles, S. 1996. "Living Arrangements of the Elderly in America, 1880–1980." In *Aging and Generational Relations over the Life Course: Historical and Cross-Cultural Perspectives,* ed. T. Hareven. Berlin: Walter de Gruyter.

Ryrie, C. C. 1982. "Biblical Teaching on Divorce and Remarriage." *Grace Theological Journal* 3 (Fall): 177–92.

Sands, S. 1995. "What is dissociated?" *Dissociation* 7:145–53.

Schremer, A. 1998. "Divorce in Papyrus Se'lim 13 Once Again: A Reply to Tal Ilan." *Harvard Theological Review* 91 (April): 193–202.

Schwalbe, R. 2008. *Sixty, Sexy and Successful.* Westport, CT: Praeger Publications.

Shea, G. F., A. Haasen. 2005. *The Older Worker Advantage.* Westport, CT: Praeger Publications.

Sheehy, G. 1995. *New Passages: Mapping Your Life Across Time.* New York: Ballantine Books.

Silverstein, M. 1995. "Stability and Change in Temporal Distance Between the Elderly and Their Children." *Demography* 32:29–45.

Simmons, H. C. Religion, Aging, and Spirituality: An Online Annotated Bibliography for Graceful Aging. Center on Aging, Union PSCE, page 1. http://gargoyle.union-psce.edu/aging/

Sloane, P. D., D. Brooker, L. Cohen, C. Douglass, P. Edelman, B. R. Fulton, S. Jarrott, et al. 2006. "Dementia Care Mapping as a Research Tool." *International Journal of Geriatric Psychiatry* 22:580–89.

Snowdon, D. 2001. *Aging With Grace: What the Nun Study Teaches Us About Leading Longer, Healthier, and More Meaningful Lives.* New York: Bantam Books.

Snyderman, N. 2007. Aging Without Children—Who Provides Care? More Americans Aren't Having Children, and Many Worry About Elder Care. *NBC News, Nightly News with Brian Williams. Msnbc.com.* May 2, 2007. http://www.msnbc.msn.com/id/18444782/ns/nightly_news_with_brian_williams-trading_places (accessed June 29, 2009)

Speare, A., and R. Avery. 1993. "Who Helps Whom in Older Parent-Child Families?" *Journal of Gerontology* 48:S64–S73.

Stibich, M. 2009. Think Positive About Aging and Live Longer. *About.com* April 26, 2009. http://longevity.about.com/od/mentalfitness/p/positive_aging.htm (accessed July 10, 2009).

Torrey, B. 1988. "Assets of the Aged: Clues and Issues." *Population and Development Review* 14:489–98.

Treas, J., and B. Logue. 1986. "Economic Development and the Older Population." *Population and Development Review* 12 (4):645–74.

U.S. Substance Abuse and Mental Health Services Administration. 2003. *Get Connected! Linking Older Adults With Medication, Alcohol and Mental Health Resources.* Washington, DC: Author.

Valsiner, J., and K. Connolly, eds. 2003. *Handbook of Developmental Psychology. Part 6: Development in Adulthood.* Thousand Oaks, CA: Sage Publications.

Vartanian, T. P., and J. M. McNamara. 2002. "Older Women in Poverty: The Impact of Midlife Factors." *Journal of Marriage and Family* 64:532–48.

Verbrugge, L. M., A. L. Gruber-Baldini, and J. L. Fozard. 1996 "Age Differences and Age Changes in Activities: Baltimore Longitudinal Study of Aging." *Journal of Gerontology* 51B:S30–S41.

Vickers-Willis, R. 2004. *Men Navigating Midlife.* Victoria, Australia: Wayfinder Publishing.

Vincent, J. 2003. Consumerism, Identity and Old Age. #5 in Old Age. New York: Routledge/Taylor & Francis Group.

Waehrer, K., and S. Crystal. 1995. "The Impact of Coresidence on Economic Well-Being of Elderly Widows." *Journal of Gerontology* 50B:S250–58.

Walker, B. 1996. *Preventing Problem Use of Alcohol, Injury Prevention for the Elderly.* Gaithersburg, MD: Aspen Publishers.

Waters, T., O. Almagor, S. Finkel, K. Harter, P. Bartolozzi, P. Mitzen, J. Lyons, P. Edelman, B. Fulton, and S. Hughes. 2001. "Understanding Costs of Home and Community Based Services." *Managed Care Quarterly* 9 (1): 45–53.

WebMD Feature. Secrets of Aging Well. *WebMD.* http://www.webmd.com/healthy-aging/features/secrets-of-aging-well (accessed July 10, 2009).

Windhorst, C. E., and Hollinger-Smith, L. M. 2005. "Mather's-More Than a Café: Providing Venues for Engagement." *The Journal on Active Aging* November/December, 43–47.

Wise, D. A. 2009. *Developments in the Economics of Aging.* Chicago: University of Chicago Press, 2009.

Wolf, D., and B. Soldo. 1988. "Household Composition Choices of Older Unmarried Women." *Demography* 25 (3): 387–403.

Women in Midlife—Security and Fulfillment (Part II), Annotated Bibliography. A Compendium of Papers Submitted to the Select Committee on Aging and the Subcommittee on Retirement Income and Employment, House of Representatives, Ninety-Fifth Congress, Second Session. ED178833.

Worobey, J. and R. Angel. 1990. "Functional Capacity and Living Arrangements of Unmarried Elderly Persons." *Journal of Gerontology* 45:S95–S101.

Worthington, B. 2009. Elder Suicide: A Needless Tragedy. *Aging Well.* http://www.agingwellmag.com/news/exclusive_03.shtml (accessed June 3, 2009).

Yaron, R. 1966. "The Restoration of Marriage." *Journal of Jewish Studies* 17:1–11.

Index

About the Author

Dr. ANGELA BROWNE-MILLER is a psychotherapist, lecturer, and consultant based in northern California. She is founder of Addiction Stoppers based in northern California, director of Metaxis® Institute also based in northern California. She has been a keynote speaker at conferences around the world on aging, human development throughout the life cycle, addiction, violence, trauma, and behavior change. She is set editor of the *Praeger International Collection on Addictions*, 4 vols (2009); set editor for the *Violence and Abuse in Society* set, 4 vols (2010); and is the author of numerous books, including *To Have and to Hurt: Seeing, Changing or Escaping Patterns of Abuse in Relationships* (2007) and also *Raising Thinking Children and Teens: Guiding Mental and Moral Development* (2009). Browne-Miller earned two doctorates and two masters degrees at the University of California, Berkeley, where she then lectured in three departments for some 14 years. She has served as a National Institute of Mental Health Postdoctoral Fellow, a U.S. Department of Public Health Fellow; Executive Consultant to Parkside Medical Services; the Research Education and Treatment Director for the Cokenders Alcohol and Drug Program; an advisor to mental health and treatment programs in the United States and several other countries; and project director on several California Department of Health violence prevention projects. She has worked in clinical and educational settings with several thousand persons. Dr. Browne-Miller is an internationally recognized expert in: issues across the life span including childhood, adolescence, college years, parenting, midlife, and aging; abuses, violences, traumas, and addictions affecting persons of all ages; and, adaptation, learning, and performance in all stages of life. She can be reached at DoctorAngela@aol.com and www.AngelaBrowne-Miller.com/